Self-Sufficiency
Soap Making

Self-Sufficiency
Soap Making

Sarah Ade

Skyhorse Publishing

Skyhorse Publishing books may be purchased in bulk at special discounts for sales promotion, corporate gifts, fund-raising, or educational purposes. Special editions can also be created to specifications. For details, contact the Special Sales Department, Skyhorse Publishing, 555 Eighth Avenue, Suite 903, New York, NY 10018 or info@skyhorsepublishing.com.

www.skyhorsepublishing.com

10 9 8 7 6 5 4 3 2

Library of Congress Cataloging-in-Publication Data

Ade, Sarah.
Soap making : self-sufficiency / Sarah Ade.
p. cm.
Includes index.
ISBN 978-1-60239-790-3 (hardcover : alk. paper)
1. Soap. I. Title.

TP991.A4 2009
668'.12--dc22
2009016031

Printed in China

CONTENTS

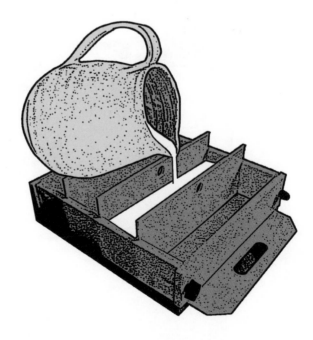

INTRODUCTION

Skin is our largest organ, but how well do we really look after it? We often think about what we put into our bodies, but how much time do we take to consider what we put *onto* our bodies?

I believe in considering mind, body, and skin as a whole. My philosophy is to make soap as "naked" as possible with no unnecessary additives, so every ingredient is beneficial to our skin.

The soaps in this book are good for you but this doesn't mean they can't look great and be wonderfully indulgent too—you don't have to go all ultra-purist and use a big block of unscented "natural" soap to be kind to your skin, yourself, and the world around you. Creating beautiful, luxurious soaps from natural ingredients is great fun, and no more difficult than making a less attractive bar.

I imagine, as you're reading this book, that you take an interest in what you put onto your body as well as what you put into your body. The pages you are about to read are packed full of helpful advice about how to make

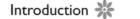

your own luxurious and beautiful soaps at home, using the best natural ingredients. You'll also have lots of fun while you're at it!

On the following pages, you will learn which ingredients to choose and their properties, how to put ingredients together for a specific purpose, the benefits of sourcing ingredients locally, and why your body will thank you for choosing holistic skin care. The recipes range from fun and frivolous to sensible and serious and include ideas for alternative soap-making methods and fun homemade skincare ideas. This is by no means an exhaustive source of recipes and information, but will hopefully be a starting point to inspire you. Perhaps once you've grasped the basics, you will create your own favorite recipes. Enjoy and indulge!

Sarah Ade

The joy of soap

Soap, in one form or another, has been with us for many centuries. Initially used purely for its cleansing qualities, soap can now be tailor-made to suit our skin and we are able to select ingredients for their conditioning properties to care for our skin, body, and mind. We can create soaps scented to perfection for whatever purpose we choose, using only the very best ingredients, and end up with a product which not only cleans but also conditions our bodies.

What is soap?

Contrary to popular opinion, soap itself does not actually clean. Soap is in fact a catalyst which helps water to wash our skin more effectively, allowing dirt to adhere to the soapy lather rather than our skin, and be rinsed away by the water. Or as my grandfather—a chemist and physicist—used to say, "Soap makes water wetter."

A brief history

Humans have used soap for thousands of years. A soap-like substance was found in ceramic containers during an excavation of ancient Babylon, dating back to around 2800 BC. At that time soap would have been made using animal fat, wood ash, and water. Mixing wood ash and water forms a caustic lye solution. Imagine a tribe of ancient people working around a camp fire. Fat spills into the ashes, and the ashes are then removed to the waste pile. Later it rains and water runs through the ashes and onto the fat. Perhaps someone grabbed a handful of ashes to scrub a cooking vessel, or maybe the run-off from the waste pile ran into a nearby stream where people were washing their clothes or themselves. It is believed that this is how the process of saponification was discovered, and humans soon began to use soap for various purposes such as bathing, washing clothes, and cleaning cooking utensils.

The chemistry of soap making

Saponification is the process by which soap is produced from a solution of oils and lye. When fatty acids mix with sodium there is a chemical reaction, the end result of which is soap. The fatty acids in the soaps included in this book are provided by butters and oils, and the sodium is in the form of sodium hydroxide (lye). When mixed together at the right temperature these ingredients react, creating soap with a by-product of glycerin (which is naturally moisturizing).

During saponification, the alkalinity of the lye is canceled out by the acidic oils, thus resulting, after four weeks of curing time, in a bar of soap which has an almost neutral pH. When cold-processed soap (the type of soap included in this book) is initially made, it is slightly caustic. For this reason you must leave soap to cure for at least 4 weeks to allow completion of the saphonification process or it may irritate the skin. Soap is often not entirely neutral—the average pH is somewhere between 8 and 9.5 (slightly alkaline)—but the soaps in this book are generally around 7.5 to 8, so quite near the neutral pH of 7. The original soap-making methods—using a lye solution made naturally with wood ash and water—would have created a soft soap quite unlike today's firm bars. This is due to the use of the active ingredient potassium hydroxide rather than sodium hydroxide, which is used in most soap making today. Potassium hydroxide is still used, however, for making liquid soaps (see pages 110–113).

Warning
Soap making is a chemical process and should be undertaken with care. Sodium hydroxide is highly caustic and dangerous if not managed properly. Keep children and pets away from your soap making area and ensure that you handle all ingredients with care.

It is difficult to measure the strength of the lye produced from wood ash and water. By using sodium hydroxide crystals (also known as caustic soda) we can be sure that the end result will be a gentle bar of soap. Using a lye solution made from wood ash may be more natural, but it will create a soap that does not harden and, if the strength of the lye is misjudged, the soap may be caustic and burn the skin.

Commercial soap making

Most commercial soaps are produced using the full-boiled method and often contain animal fats in the form of sodium tallowate. The full-boiled method involves boiling the fats and lye together while mixing until they saponify. Due to the high temperatures, saponification can happen in a matter of hours rather than the weeks it takes a cold-processed soap to fully saponify. Once saponified, the mixture undergoes a number of stages to remove any excess lye and to neutralize the soap. The glycerin produced during the saponification process is separated out and often sold to the cosmetics industry. The end result is a plain soap to which a variety of extra ingredients are added. The soap is melted down and fragrance, color, fillers (to add more weight to the soap), builders (such as water softeners, exfoliators, and synthetic detergents), skin conditioners, and other ingredients are added.

Artificial detergents and your skin

Many of the products we use to clean our skin are not soap at all but are in fact chemical detergents or a mixture of detergents and soap. These products often claim to be kinder to your skin than soap, and may even state that they are pH neutral or at the skin's own slightly acidic pH level of 5.5. To achieve this pH numerous chemicals are added to the products. When hand-making soap there is no need to add these chemicals as you can achieve a pH close to neutral using a process known as superfatting. This involves adding extra oils and butters which do not saponify, and so are left unchanged by the soap making process. These butters and oils are then able to moisturize and nourish your skin. Fats are acidic, so adding these extra fats reduces the pH, bringing the finished soap closer to the skin's natural level.

Why make your own?

When making soap at home you have complete control over what goes into your soap and the processes you use to make it. You can make soaps to suit individual requirements, make different shapes using molds, create stamps to emboss designs, mix colors using natural ingredients, and vary the fragrance to suit your mood. Inventing new and exciting soaps is great fun and can become a real addiction!

The benefits of homemade soap

If you walk into the kitchen when someone is making homemade, natural soap you could easily be forgiven for thinking they are baking a cake or making fudge. The processes are somewhat similar—oils and butters are carefully weighed out then heated gently on the stove in heavy saucepans or measured into large jugs or bowls. Delicious ingredients are carefully combined and poured into molds and trays. The colors are rich and natural—golden caramels, light creams, chocolate browns, deep greens, and earthy purples.

After a couple of days, when the mixture has hardened, the soaps are gently pressed from the trays and cut into their individual blocks like big slabs of cheese, or popped out of their molds like little carvings. Then they must cure, lightly covered, in a warm room where air can circulate around them. And, like cheese, they need time to mature. They really do look good enough to eat.

So what is it that makes homemade soap so special? A major benefit is that you can choose exactly what you want to go into your soap. The ingredients for each soap include a carefully selected blend of base oils, butters, and essential oils. These can be specific to a particular skin type and personality or to a specific task such as cleaning stubborn ground-in dirt or nourishing chapped hands. Whatever purpose you choose to make soap for, it is worth researching each of the base oils and butters in the ingredients list to find out which will suit your skin and personality before choosing which soap to make.

After using your handmade soap, your skin should feel soft and supple, not dry and tight as skin often does after using commercial tallow-based soaps, and you are bound to love the rich lather and longevity of your homemade soaps. You may even find that you prefer not to use commercial soaps anymore. Many people who revert back to commercially-produced soaps find that their skin feels tight and irritated and their hair lackluster and dry. It also doesn't take a lot of time or money to keep a family (and a few friends too) supplied with high-quality natural soap—and the benefits are plentiful and visible, giving you instant satisfaction.

The cold-process method

The technique most often used for homemade soap, and which we will be using in this book, is called the cold-process method. Cold-processing involves heating the butters and oils to somewhere between 80 and 100°F—just hot enough to melt them and to start the saponification process. If oils are heated above 104°F they begin to degrade and can become carcinogenic. Other soap-making techniques involve higher temperatures to quicken the saponification process, but keeping the temperature low retains the properties of the oils and butters. Homemade soaps made using the cold-process method have a soft, creamy lather thanks to the rich oils and butters used, and are also long-lasting.

Shortcuts and other techniques

The cold-process method is not the only technique for making soap at home, but the soaps produced using alternative methods are not made from scratch and therefore cannot legitimately be called homemade. That said, some techniques, such as re-milling, can be very handy for recycling soap scraps and you'll find the method for this on pages 98–99 as well as a recipe for melt and pour soap, using ready-made soap bases, on pages 100–101. A brief overview of some other techniques you might like to try, such as making transparent, liquid, and whipped soaps, can be found on pages 102–113.

Animal fats

All of the ingredients for every recipe in this book are vegetarian and nearly all (except for beeswax, milk, and honey) are vegan. Some people may not like the idea of putting animal fat onto their skin, but if you would prefer to be totally self-sufficient, using locally- or home-produced animal fat, then refer to the saponification chart on pages 124–125 to work out the amount of lye you will need for the type of fat you are using.

A holistic approach

Followers of holism view the body as a whole rather than as a number of parts. Holistic medicine works within this philosophy, by finding and treating the cause of the problem rather than concentrating on the symptom. Taking a holistic view, our skin is intrinsically linked to the rest of our body and it therefore makes sense to treat it with care and kindness.

We are whole

Our body is one unit made up of what we often consider to be separate parts—our physical body (skin, hair, internal organs, and bones), and our mental body (the mind and soul). We rarely look at the whole, but all of our body parts are interlinked and if one is compromised the rest of our being will suffer the knock-on effects. If you are overweight, unfit, or eat a poor diet you may become depressed as your mind responds to your physical body's poor health. On the other hand if your body is fed with healthy, vital foods, kept fit and active, and your skin is clean and chemical free, the odds are that you will feel happy, exuberant, and full of life.

Holism and the skin

If we use products that are full of artificial ingredients and chemicals on our skin, we are likely to feel the effects of these chemicals and suffer both physical and psychological reactions. Consider for instance how a nicotine patch works. This is a transdermal patch designed to be placed on the skin to deliver a specific dose of medication through the skin and into the bloodstream. The advantage in using a transdermal patch for people trying to quit smoking is that it allows a controlled release of nicotine over a period of time, thus alleviating cigarette cravings by allowing the body to absorb nicotine topically (through the skin) over the course of the day.

When we consider that topical applications of medication are well known within most societies in one form or another, you'd think it would be common knowledge that our skin directly absorbs much of what we put onto it, and what it absorbs affects our whole being. But when we buy perfumes, make-up, skin and body care products we tend to make choices based on how these products smell, feel, and look rather than what they contain and how their ingredients may affect us. By looking at ourselves holistically, and also at the products we are putting into and onto our bodies, we can take control of our overall health.

Of course, some of us are more sensitive than others and many of you are probably saying, "But my skin is fine, and my health is fine. I don't have any problems with the products I use." Our bodies have an incredible ability to adapt and to heal. Today many of us survive on a diet very far removed from that which our bodies are suited to, and yet our bodies manage to siphon out necessary nutrients even from a diet heavy in sugar, salt, and fat-rich processed foods. But as we get older the stress we put on our system becomes more apparent, and little trifles become bigger health issues. A bit of dry skin becomes psoriasis or eczema, the occasional headache progresses to a migraine, and a slight upset stomach develops into a full-blown food allergy. Why not take control of your body—and your life—by becoming more aware of these issues and choosing to consume healthy foods and use natural and holistic skin care before you begin to suffer the negative effects of a toxic lifestyle?

Did you know...
...that we are constantly renewing our cells and that the body completely renews itself every seven years, so it pays to give our body the building blocks it needs to create healthy new cells, and a healthy new body!

Many people suffer from skin complaints, bouts of depression, allergies, headaches, and other conditions which are often not serious enough to warrant a trip to the doctor but can lower their quality of life nonetheless. These health problems can be a reaction to the chemical cocktail we subject our bodies to daily in the form of skin care products, washing detergents, and household cleaners. Why not take the first step towards better health by cutting out artificial skin care products? And what better place to start than with the most basic—the soap we use to clean our skin. It is empowering to take your health and well-being into your own hands and realize that you have ultimate control over what you think and how you feel, and you can start to make the changes necessary for a healthier, happier life right now.

Using ingredients holistically

As well as being concerned with treating the body as a whole, holism also involves using the whole of a product, either to eat or to apply externally. This includes whole grains, vegetables with their skins on (either organic or thoroughly washed to help remove harmful pesticides), and whole fruits (although freshly squeezed juice is good for us and tastes great, it's not as good as eating the whole fruit). The less processed and the closer to their natural state, the better the products are for us.

If you look on the labels of many so-called natural skin care products you will see ingredients such as limonene, citranool, and linalool listed. These are isolated components of natural essential oils, so they are classified as "natural" ingredients.

However, they are far from holistic, and have usually lost any therapeutic value the original essential oil held. In isolation, these ingredients, mostly used as fragrances, are incredibly strong and can irritate the skin. To give you an example of just how strong they are: Limonene, often used to give a pleasant citrus smell to "natural" cosmetics and skin care products, also works as a paint stripper. And linalool, used in skin care products for its floral, spicy aroma, is also used in the pest control industry as an insecticide. Although the amount of these ingredients used in skin care products is tiny compared with the amounts used for industrial purposes, they are added purely to make the product smell nice, and not because they have any beneficial value for your skin or your health. When making skin care products at home, you choose what ingredients to add. You can make your products smell wonderful using totally natural, whole, skin-friendly ingredients.

A great way to introduce some of the principles of holism into the soapmaking process is to use fresh herbs, plants, and flowers. You can do this by creating an oil or water infusion (see pages 48–49) or by adding petals, whole flowers, buds, or chopped leaves to your soap mixture. When sourcing essential oils, base oils, and butters, ensure the provider can guarantee their products are 100 percent natural and are as unrefined as possible.

A macrobiotic lifestyle

The word macrobiotic comes from *macrobiota*, a medical term for a region's living organisms (flora and fauna) that are large enough to be seen with the naked eye. However macro comes from the Greek *makros*, meaning not only large but also long. So the principal philosophy behind a macrobiotic diet and lifestyle is that it is inductive of a long life.

In a general context, the term macrobiotic has come to represent a specific type of diet and lifestyle, one that largely involves choosing locally-produced foods, therefore using the *macrobiota* of your local area. A macrobiotic approach to food recognizes that the quality of the food we consume can impact on our health and general well-being. It suggests choosing natural and unprocessed foods, using traditional methods of preparing food, and focusing on whole foods which are locally grown and seasonal.

The philosophy of living macrobiotically can be widened to include the way we care for our skin and body. As previously discussed, our health rests not just on the nutrients we consume but also on the nutrients and toxins that our body absorbs through our skin. One of the key principles of macrobiotics, as a diet or a lifestyle choice, is to use locally grown ingredients whenever possible—the closer to home, the better. The idea behind this principle is that the minerals, trace elements, vitamins, and nutrients your body needs when living in a certain area can usually be found close to home. At different times of the year our body will have different requirements and by using seasonal produce we can provide for these needs.

Keep it local

When you start to source ingredients locally you suddenly take notice of who is producing what in your area. What are the fields around you used for? What is grown in those greenhouses you drive past every day? Is there a plant nursery nearby where they grow fresh herbs? Where can you buy the meat from the sheep that live on the hill behind your house? Even in cities it is possible to find out about vegetable box schemes or investigate allotment produce. One of the huge benefits of sourcing your ingredients locally, both for use internally and externally, is that you can actually interact with the producer. You can visit a provider and talk to them directly to ensure the ingredients are being grown or raised in a way you are happy with. Once you get into the habit of sourcing locally and using seasonal ingredients, a whole new world opens up!

Wild and home grown

Fresh ingredients such as flowers and herbs can easily be grown in the garden, on a balcony, or even on a window sill. An even easier way to get hold of healthy, local, natural, and seasonal produce is to use the abundance of wild plants growing all around us. This is a great way of sourcing local produce if you don't have the time or the space to grow your own, or if you just don't have green fingers. Hedge row shopping is a wonderful activity and, with a good reference book as your guide, you will be amazed at the wild herbs and plants out there that can be used in your kitchen, both for cooking and for skin care. However make sure you pick away from roads as vegetation there will have absorbed pollution from passing vehicles.

Warning
Take extreme care when foraging for wild ingredients and always refer to a reference book for identification purposes. Some wild plants can be toxic to humans and animals. If you are in any doubt as to the plant's identity, leave it alone.

Self-sufficiency

Being self-sufficient is all about using what we have around us and not relying on the outside world too much. This includes everything we have covered so far, from sourcing local and seasonal produce to growing your own ingredients. Making your own soap and skin care products can be an extremely satisfying activity in the self-sufficiency stakes. I would say that the first act on a path to self-sufficiency is to take control of your diet, growing the foods you would like to consume in a manner you are happy with. And the second is to take control of your skin care, making the products which will come into contact with your skin from scratch so you know exactly what goes into them. From here you can go on to gain control, other aspects of your life, but these are a good first and second base. This way your health is under your control once and for all. When you start thinking about making your own skin care products, you will probably discover that a lot of the items you currently use are actually unnecessary. "The simpler the better" is a rule I like to stick to, and if you can create a soap that is nourishing and moisturizing as well as cleansing, who needs additional moisturizers and conditioners? Getting back to nature is a real feel-good process—a lifestyle spring clean!

A note about organic produce

The fact that organic produce is now so readily available is a wonderful thing, and I am sure it is helping to make all our lives healthier. But remember that just because something is organic does not necessarily make it good for us, or even more ethical. For instance, you can get organic white sugar but we all know that the less-refined brown sugar is better for us. On the other hand organic producers in general tend to be more conscientious about their products and production methods. Use your judgment when considering whether to buy organic and always choose the healthiest and most natural products available.

Sourcing ethical palm oil

As you will see, palm oil is used in many of the recipes in this book. It has been highlighted in the media that palm oil production in many countries is destructive and unethical. In parts of Indonesia, for instance, large swathes of tropical rainforest have been cut down to grow oil palm trees. Obviously we don't want precious rainforests to be destroyed so that we can make a bar of soap, so I urge you to source ethical palm oil. I buy organic Colombian palm oil produced through a scheme in which palm oil plantations replace cocoa plantations (this is the plant used to produce cocaine), so no virgin rainforest is cut down. When buying palm oil always ask where it has come from and how it was produced.

The essentials

In order to make soap at home you don't need any fancy equipment, just some basic tools from your kitchen. You may even find that you already have many of the ingredients in your kitchen cupboard or garden. One of the most wonderful things about making your own soap is that you can choose which ingredients to add—if you love the smell of a particular rose in summer, why not use it to make soap? Have fun with your soap and use your imagination to create a natural, wholesome bar for you and your family to enjoy.

Ingredients

All of the ingredients listed below will benefit your skin when added to your homemade soap. Some also have other desirable properties such as giving your soap a pleasant color, making it smell nice, or helping to achieve a particular texture. This is by no means a comprehensive list of the ingredients you can use to make soap at home but is a good starting point.

Base oils and butters

You can use any oil or fat to make soap. Butters or fats are really just oils that are solid at room temperature. The saponification process deodorizes most oils so the smell of the finished soap won't resemble the oil or fat used to make it. If you want to use oils, butters, or fats not included here you can refer to the saponification chart on pages 124–125 to find out how much lye you will need. However, it would be a good idea to research the properties of these ingredients before use to ensure they are suitable for achieving the particular soap you want to make.

You must have a certain percentage of saturated and unsaturated oils and fats in your soap or it will not saponify properly. For this reason it is impossible to make a firm soap using only hemp seed oil, for instance, as this is an unsaturated oil. Most vegetable oils are not 100 percent saturated or unsaturated but have a higher percentage of one or the other. In general unsaturated oils are liquid at room temperature and are more unstable (have a tendency to go rancid quickly) and saturated oils are solid at room temperature and are stable (and don't go rancid so quickly). As a general rule, at least 25 percent of the oils and fats in your recipe should be saturated to create a firm bar of soap.

To stop the superfatted oils in your soap from going rancid I would recommend adding grapefruit seed extract, rosemary extract, or vitamin E oil as a natural anti-oxidant and preservative to lengthen the life of your soaps. In this book I focus on grapefruit seed extract as this is what I generally use, but I have listed the properties of both rosemary extract (see page 43) and vitamin E oil (see page 42) in case you would like to create your own recipe using these ingredients. If you are using mainly saturated fats in a recipe it may not be necessary to add a preservative, but it does no harm so you may as well add some anyway just in case. Rancid soap is not bad for you as such, but it smells horrible and the oils lose their beneficial qualities, so the longer a shelf life you can give your soap naturally, the better.

Oils

Apricot seed oil (unsaturated) comes from the nut inside an apricot pit. Next time you eat an apricot, crack the pit (not with your teeth!) and inside you will find a small, almond-shaped seed. This is in fact very similar to an almond, and is often used in almond products such as Italian Amaretti biscuits. Apricot seeds are good to eat, tasting very similar to almonds, and are high in vitamin B17 which is thought to help prevent cancer. From these seeds a light emollient oil is produced. This oil is both skin softening and moisturizing. It is easily absorbed by the skin and, when used in soap making, creates a conditioning, stable lather.

Avocado oil (unsaturated) originated in Mexico where the avocado was prized by the Aztecs as a health-enhancing fruit due to its high nutritional content, and also as a skin care ingredient for its emollient qualities. The oil is produced from the oil-rich fruit of the avocado and extracted using either solvents or a centrifugal method. (The oil produced through the centrifugal method is of a higher quality and more natural as it has not come into contact with harsh solvents.) Avocado oil is cholesterol and trans fatty acid–free and contains the omegas 3 and 6 which the body needs as building blocks for everything from your brain to your skin and hair. The oil has nourishing, hydrating, and regenerating properties and deeply penetrates the epidermis, leaving no oily residue on the skin.

Castor oil (unsaturated) is a unique oil made from the castor bean. Castor oil was valued highly by the ancient Egyptians who used it as a lamp oil and was a popular laxative in the 1950s, often given to babies and children to improve their health. The castor bean is rich in ricinoleic acid (unique to the castor bean) which has analgesic and anti-inflammatory qualities. When used on the skin this oil is very moisturizing as it is a humectant (attracts moisture to itself and holds it), sealing moisture in and helping to retain moisture levels in the skin, scalp, and hair. It is a great addition to shampoo bars and dog soaps as it conditions the hair follicles while the soap cleanses. This oil also gives soap a slightly translucent quality.

Coconut oil (saturated) is solid at room temperature and is therefore also known as coconut butter. It is usually made from the dried flesh of the coconut. When it is produced from the fresh flesh it is known as virgin coconut oil. This oil is commonly used in the food industry for making products such as margarine, non-dairy creamers, and for cooking as it has a high smoke point. In India coconut oil is often used to condition the hair and scalp. In soap making it creates a nice firm soap with a good lather and loads of suds. These suds are what helps water to clean our skin, so coconut oil gives soap a wonderful cleansing quality. Even though this oil gives us a great fluffy lather, don't be tempted to add too much as in too high a proportion it can have a drying effect on the skin. (See Coconut Milk on page 43 for more about the properties of coconuts.)

Hemp seed oil (unsaturated) is extracted from raw hemp seeds and contains beneficial fatty acids. Hemp seed oil is high in essential fatty acids, vitamins, and minerals which feed you and your skin. This rich but light oil has numerous remarkable benefits—it is moisturizing; anti-inflammatory; aids healing; can help skin conditions such as acne, eczema, and psoriasis; and encourages hair to repair. In soap making it creates a very gentle and nourishing soap which is great to use on the face as well as the body. This oil is also very good for you when eaten raw (most oils lose their beneficial qualities when used for cooking due to high temperatures) and makes a delicious and nutritious salad dressing.

Neem oil (unsaturated) is made from the seeds of the neem tree. It is popular in India where it is renowned for its healing properties and has been termed the "oil of wonder." Neem oil is known for its antiseptic qualities and for its effectiveness in treating skin conditions such as acne, eczema, psoriasis, burns, and ulcers. Due to its antiseptic, antibacterial, and anti-fungal qualities it is very effective at fighting infection and can ease chronic skin conditions. It is also an effective natural insecticide and can be mixed with water and sprayed on house plants as a safe alternative to chemical pesticides.

Olive oil (unsaturated) is extracted from the fruit of the olive tree. It is one of the best-known oils in natural soap making and a soap with an olive oil base is referred to as castile soap, from the area of Castile in France where this type of soap originated.

Olive oil is so good for the skin that in my grandmother's day, mothers used to cover their babies with olive oil before putting them in the bath to protect the baby's sensitive skin from the drying effects of soap and water. It was used in much the same way as we use baby oil today. Commercial baby oil, however, is a mineral oil and mineral oils actually dry the skin. They work by trapping moisture rather than replenishing the skin's natural oils and are potentially harmful to children if consumed and extremely dangerous if taken into the lungs. Olive oil, however, is a vegetable oil and is moisturizing and nourishing to the skin. It has also commonly been used to encourage hair and eyelashes to grow thick and strong. Olive oil is a wonderful base oil in soaps as it is gentle and kind to the skin—if it can be used directly on newborn babies' skins, it must be one of the most skin-friendly oils around. It is also very stable for an unsaturated oil, thus creating a long-lasting bar of soap as well as being affordable and readily available.

Palm oil (saturated) is a solid oil made from the fruit of the oil palm tree. Palm oil should not be confused with palm seed oil which is made from the seed of the fruit and has different properties. It is commonly used in the production of foods such as margarine and chocolate. In soap making it creates a good, hard bar with a stable lather and is often used instead of tallow, its traditional equivalent, for this purpose, sometimes being referred to as vegetable tallow. (See page 23 for a note on sourcing ethical palm oil.)

Sweet almond oil (unsaturated) is obtained from the dried seeds of the almond tree, or what we commonly eat as dried almonds. The plant is closely related to the peach and apricot, and apricot seed oil and sweet almond oil have very similar properties. It is a light emollient oil which both softens and moisturizes the skin. This is a popular oil for use during aromatherapy massages as it has a fine, light texture that is steadily absorbed by the skin, giving time to complete a massage before the oil sinks in leaving the skin smooth and non-greasy. In soap this light and versatile oil creates a conditioning, stable lather.

Thistle (safflower) oil (unsaturated) is derived from the thistle (or safflower) plant. Traditionally cultivated for its seeds, which are used for coloring and flavoring foods and making red and yellow dyes, it has more recently been grown for its oil which is used in the food industry similarly to sunflower oil. Packed full of essential fatty acids, making up 80 percent of the oil's content, this is a wonderfully nourishing oil. It is great for oily skin and generally good for skin conditions due to its dry nature. It keeps for up to two years if stored out of direct sunlight and is light and easily absorbed by the skin. Like hemp seed oil it's also delicious in salad dressings, so it's good for you both inside and out! The pretty yellow flowers are sometimes used in cooking as substitute for saffron. The seed is a popular alternative to sunflower seeds for bird feeders as the nutritional qualities are similar, but these seeds are less likely to be eaten by squirrels.

Butters

These wonderfully moisturizing butters will help to create a luxuriously pampering bar of soap, not to mention smelling good enough to eat too!

Cocoa butter (saturated) is obtained from cocoa beans, the by-product of this process being cocoa powder. Cocoa butter is used in the confectionery industry to make chocolate and other sweets and cakes. In skin care it is an extremely moisturizing butter which is easily absorbed by the skin. Cocoa butter is used all over the world as a skin softener, although it can be pretty hard if not mixed with some softer butters or oils. One of its most well-known properties is as an easer of stretch-marks and other skin blemishes. When used in soaps, cocoa butter creates a rich, nourishing, firm bar that lasts and lasts.

Mango butter (saturated) is extracted from the seed kernels of the tropical mango fruit. It is non-greasy and is easily absorbed into the skin, has emollient properties, and can speed up healing. It is also thought to provide natural protection against UV radiation. Mango butter has traditionally been used in the rainforests and tropics for its skin-softening, soothing, moisturizing, and protective properties, as well as to restore flexibility to the skin and reduce degeneration of skin cells.

Shea butter (saturated) comes from the shea nut, found inside the fruit of the karite or shea tree and it is sometimes also referred to as karite butter. As well as being beneficial to the skin as a moisturizer, softener, and soother, it is also edible and is sometimes used in the confectionery industry to replace cocoa butter in chocolate. This soft butter has such great moisturizing properties that it is often used to improve the appearance of scars, stretch marks, burns, and rashes. Shea butter also provides protection against the sun's harmful UV rays, although this quality varies.

Essential oils

Using just a small amount of an essential oil in a carefully chosen blend allows your body to utilize the aromatherapy and herbal properties necessary for your health and well-being without overpowering your body and overloading your senses. For this reason, only a very small amount of any one essential oil is used in the recipes in this book.

Warning
Don't get carried away with essential oils. They are strong and should be handled with respect. Always read any warnings on the packaging before use. The amount of essential oils included in any soap should be less than 5 percent and 2–3 percent is usually adequate. The suggested amount for each recipe in this book is well below the 5 percent limit.

Benzoin has a sweet, warm aroma. This resinous oil has a great calming and uplifting effect on the mind and is said to help comfort the sad and lonely. On a physical level it boosts circulation, helps ease respiratory disorders, increases the skin's elasticity, and soothes irritated skin.

Cedarwood has a deep, woody aroma and is antiseptic and astringent. It also calms the nerves and helps boost the circulation.

Cinnamon is a warm, spicy oil that fights exhaustion and feelings of depression and weakness. It also has powerful anti-rheumatic properties and can help to fight colds and flu. It is analgesic and antiseptic and the powdered spice can be sprinkled directly onto minor abrasions.

Citronella is a sharp, strong-smelling oil renowned for its insect-repelling qualities. It is also great for clearing the mind and softening the skin and can help to combat oily skin and sweaty feet.

Clary sage is a soothing oil with a wonderful heavy, heady aroma. It helps to de-stress the mind and is said to be an antidepressant. On a more physical level it is antiseptic, antibacterial, astringent, and an aphrodisiac. It can also be used as a natural deodorant. A great relaxant for aching muscles and tired minds, in large quantities it is soporific.

Clove stimulates the mind and lifts depression while aiding digestion and easing respiratory problems. It is also an analgesic and is traditionally used for toothache.

Frankincense has been prized for centuries and at one time was as valuable as gold. It is wonderfully rejuvenating and promotes the formation of new skin cells, and for this reason it is used in many beauty creams. It has a heavy, woody aroma and is often used to aid meditation, allowing the mind to drift away.

Ginger is a warming essential oil often used for digestive problems as well as nausea including morning sickness and travel upset. It can help ease the symptoms of colds, flu, catarrhal lung conditions, and rheumatic pain. Ginger can also help heal and disperse bruising on the skin.

Lavender is renowned for its relaxing qualities. The aroma of lavender soothes the mind and calms the soul, and is good for headaches and to aid sleep. Lavender is also very healing—in the 1920s the founder of modern aromatherapy, French chemist René-Maurice Gattefossé, discovered the healing power of lavender by accident when he burned himself while carrying out an experiment. He plunged his hand into the first available fluid, which happened to be a vat of lavender oil, and was amazed at how quickly his hand healed.

Did you know...
...that lavender helps relax the mind and can help you sleep? Put a drop of lavender essential oil onto a tissue or handkerchief and place inside your pillowcase for a restful night's slumber.

Lemon rejuvenates the mind and lifts the soul, and is also said to help us be more decisive. The essential oil has a tonic effect on the circulation and is often used to treat varicose veins, poor circulation, high blood pressure, and fluid retention. It is astringent and helps to combat greasy skin.

Lemongrass is a sweet, lemony, fresh-smelling oil that revitalizes tired bodies and minds, as well as keep cellulite at bay. It has a tonic effect on the nervous system and is a gentle pain reliever and antidepressant. Good for headaches, lethargy, and poor muscle tone it also helps reduce excess perspiration. Also an effective skin toner.

Lime is a strong, invigorating citrus oil that can help lift depression and lighten your mood when you're feeling blue or out of sorts. Physically it is used to fight cellulite and to tone the skin.

Mandarin is a great aid for insomnia, stress, and nervous tension. When inhaled, it has an uplifting effect on the mind and when used on the skin, it boosts circulation and discourages water retention. Also good to help reduce marks on the skin caused by acne, scars, and stretch marks and useful for discouraging spots.

May chang has a sweet, citrus, fruity fragrance that brings with it stimulating, tonic, and antidepressant properties.

Neroli is a traditional Eastern aphrodisiac. As with lavender, this essential oil not only has great therapeutic properties but it also smells incredible. It has a relaxing effect on the body and mind and a wonderfully rejuvenating and regenerative effect on the skin, helping to prevent scarring and stretch marks.

Nutmeg is a highly aromatic oil. Warming, stimulating, and rejuvenating, it is good for calming the nerves.

Patchouli has a deep, earthy scent that is calming, grounding, and seems to banish lethargy and sharpen the wits. It's most outstanding feature is the binding action it has on skin due to strong astringent properties which can be helpful for loose skin, especially after dieting.
It also helps to regenerate tissue, cools inflammation, and heals rough, cracked skin.

Peppermint is a refreshing and stimulating oil that is also an expectorant, so helps clear out your lungs when they are a little plugged up. It helps to relieve muscle and joint pain and headaches.

Petitgrain is one of the three oils obtained from the orange tree (the others are neroli from the flowers and sweet orange from the rind of the fruit) and is extracted from the leaves. This crisp and clear essential oil boosts the conscious, intellectual side of the mind while calming stress and anxiety. It also helps to clear greasy skin and fight blemishes.

Sandalwood is a slightly spicy, woody, richly scented oil which is known to have healing properties for dry and chapped skin. The aroma is calming and uplifting. It encourages wound healing and helps with skin problems such as acne, psoriasis, and eczema. Even shaving rash will benefit from its soothing, rehydrating, and antiseptic action.

Sandalwood's fragrance can help banish depression and anxiety and calms the nervous system.

Sweet orange is a zingy, revitalizing essential oil that brings cheer and happiness to the mind. To the body it brings happiness in the form of helping dry, irritated, and problem-prone skin to cope with the trials of everyday life. Sweet orange essential oil helps to fight chills, bronchitis, colds, and flu and also helps ease nervous tension and insomnia.

Tea tree is a powerful natural antiseptic that is also antifungal, antibacterial, antiviral, and anti-inflammatory. Probably best known for its beneficial effect on acne-prone skin, there are many tea tree products available to help clear spotty teenage skin. Tea tree can be applied directly to spots, but make sure to test for allergies first on a sensitive area of skin that is not your face, such as the wrist or inside of the elbow.

Thyme has a strong, pungent aroma which aids concentration and focus. It is also an excellent bronchial and lung stimulant, making it valuable for easing bronchitis, coughs, colds, asthma, and the like. Thyme's warming qualities are great for rheumatism, sciatica, arthritis, and gout.

Ylang ylang is an extremely fragrant essential oil which has a calming effect on the mind and body and has aphrodisiac qualities, so is often used in sensuous massage oils. It also has a wonderfully balancing and stimulating effect on the skin.

Absolutes

Absolutes are highly concentrated oils derived from essential oils. However unlike linalools and limonenes (see page 18) they retain many beneficial elements of the essential oils they are derived from. You only need about one drop for every three you would use of an essential oil.

Frangipani is a tropical flower, known sometimes as West Indian Jasmine. Frangipani is also known as the "tree of life" in India because a cut branch will continue to flower and, if planted, will grow into a new tree. In Mexico, the frangipani flower is often used in healing salves and ointments. It has a heavy, sweet, tropical aroma with deeper spicy background notes reminiscent of honey or almonds.

Vanilla has been used as an aphrodisiac since the ancient times of the Aztecs. It has a warm, soothing, homely aroma which calms the emotions and eases tension. It may also be used to aid weight loss as its smell, which is reminiscent of chocolate or cookies, is said to suppress the appetite.

CO$_2$ Extractions

Carbon dioxide extraction uses CO$_2$ liquid as a solvent to extract essential oils. It is inert and so leaves no residue in the oil, and as no heat is involved in the process the oils are often of a very high quality. Some may be quite thick and need warming up before use. Coffee is the most common CO$_2$ extraction used in soap making but if you wish to use others it would be wise to research their properties first.

Coffee is said to aid in the healing of burns and scalds when applied to the skin. The aroma of coffee lifts the spirit and eases the mind. When used in soap making, coffee helps to remove kitchen smells from your hands.

Infusions

An infusion is the solution obtained when steeping or soaking something, usually in water but sometimes in oil. See pages 48–49 for information on making and using infusions in soap making.

Alkanet root was popular for skin care use in the middle ages and creates a lavender-blue color in soaps. When infused in olive oil it is a rich crimson, but once added to the soap mixture it reacts in a similar way to litmus paper and turns it blue.

Black tea creates a dark caramel color and is renowned for its antibacterial and astringent qualities. Used black tea bags placed over the eyes are also a traditional cure for puffy eyes (usually after a heavy night out!).

Calendula gives soap a golden yellow color. Due to its natural healing properties calendula has traditionally been used as an ointment on cuts, scalds, grazes, and other surface wounds. The petals can add dashes of color too when mixed through your soap.

Camomile is reputed for its healing qualities and is anti-bacterial and analgesic. It calms skin conditions and irritation, helps with headaches, eases restlessness, and helps to promote sleep. The flowers can be used to add interesting texture to your soap.

Green tea creates a light caramel color in soap and is renowned in the Orient for its antibacterial and antioxidizing properties. Tests have shown that when applied to the skin it may inhibit skin cancers caused by harmful UVB radiation. Many cosmetic and pharmaceutical companies supplement their skin care products with green tea extracts.

Other great ingredients

Beeswax is sometimes used in soap making to make a harder bar but should be used with care as it can be a skin irritant. For this reason beeswax should never make up more than 25 percent of your soap recipe. Check the saponification chart on pages 124–125 for the amount of sodium hydroxide needed.

Cocoa powder creates a rich, deep brown soap and can be mildly exfoliating when used in large quantities.

Coconut milk (and cream) is rich and full of protein. For many years coconuts have been integral to life in many tropical climates, providing nutrition from their meat and milk, hydration from coconut water, and coconut oil to nourish the skin and hair. It has been found that the unique form of saturated fat found in coconuts can actually prevent heart disease and hardening of the arteries as, unlike other saturated fats, it contains a large amount of lauric acid. Lauric acid is found in human breast milk and is what makes it so easily digestible. Coconut oil helps protect the skin against blemishes and premature aging, and may even help to reduce the risk of skin cancer.

Desiccated coconut creates a gently exfoliating soap and provides all of the beneficial qualities of coconut (see Coconut milk above).

Dried calendula petals add lovely bright yellow flecks to your soap (see page 39 for properties).

Flowers and buds such as rose, camomile, and lavender can be dried (either as open flowers or as buds) for use in your soaps. You can keep the flowers whole or scatter petals throughout your soap. Rose and camomile work well in re-milled soap but not so well in cold-processed soaps as they tend to discolor during the saponification process. However calendula petals keep their color well. It is worth experimenting with other flowers to see how well they retain their color.

Garden herbs can be added freely to your soaps. Finely chop before use for a more attractive bar as the saponification process often discolors herbs and larger pieces may not look as nice. Some herbs retain their color better than others so it is worth experimenting to see which works best.

Grapefruit seed extract is a strong antioxidant and is the preservative I suggest using in the soap recipes in this book. This oil also has many benefits for the skin as it is a natural detoxifier. It also enhances and supports the immune system due to its high levels of vitamin C and E and bioflavonoids.

Ground almonds are rich in protein, zinc, potassium, iron, B vitamins, and magnesium, so adding ground almonds to your soap allows your skin to benefit from these qualities as well as harness the moisturizing qualities of sweet almond oil. The texture of ground almonds creates a gentle exfoliating soap. Ground almonds used on a damp face make a great facial scrub, especially for teenage skin, helping to slough away dead skin cells while adding natural sweet almond oil to moisturize. This treatment is great for acne-prone skin.

Ground pumice is a natural soft pit which makes a fine powder that is great for creating an exfoliating soap as it has a gentle abrasive action.

Honey is replenishing and full of natural antibiotic and antiseptic qualities. You can use any honey to make soap, but if you can find some that is locally produced by free range bees, all the better.

Lavender buds contain healing lavender oil (see page 34) and are also mildly exfoliating while creating pretty speckles in your soap.

Lemon verbena is an aromatic herb with astringent properties. Its antibacterial and antiseptic qualities make it an effective treatment for acne, boils, and cysts. The scent of lemon verbena is calming and de-stressing, relaxing to the mind. It is also good for alleviating insomnia. It helps reduce skin puffiness and can be used as a hair tonic. The herb can be added to soaps in fresh or dried form or an infusion made using the leaves of the plant.

Milk is wonderful for replenishing and moisturizing. Cleopatra bathed in ass' milk and we too can bathe in milk and reap the benefits! The addition of milk creates a soap which is pale to dark caramel in color and the cooler the temperature, the lighter the soap. Goats' milk and sheeps' milk create a lighter soap than cows' milk because cows' milk contains higher levels of carotene. (See Making milk soaps on page 51.)

Natural spring water or distilled water is used in soap making rather than tap water (unless yours comes from a spring) as the chemicals and minerals in most tap water can affect your soap. Chlorine and minerals which make tap water "hard" may prevent your soap from turning out the way you intended.

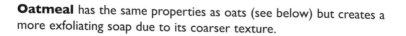

Oatmeal has the same properties as oats (see below) but creates a more exfoliating soap due to its coarser texture.

Oats condition and moisturize the skin and are an effective emollient. When added directly, oats create a gently exfoliating soap. However, to harness their great benefits without the exfoliating qualities soak the oats in cold water then drain over a bowl using a piece of cheesecloth or an old tea towel. The oat-infused water can be used to replace a portion of the water in your soap recipe. (See pages 48–49 for more on making and using infusions.) Oats also make a great face wash. To condition and exfoliate the face place some oats in a flannel and hold or tie it closed, then massage the flannel gently over your face using small circular movements. You'll soon feel the smooth oat water coming through the cloth to soothe and condition your skin.

Orris root is used as a fixative in perfumes, soap making, and other cosmetics. The orris is a type of iris and the powder, which is made from the dried root, develops a unique scent as it ages which is similar to that of violets. Essential oil can also be extracted from the dried root. The powdered root is used in toothpastes, breath fresheners, face and body powders, and food flavorings. In soap making and natural skin care it can help to fix scents.

Rosemary extract is well known for its strong antioxidant properties which help to prevent the soap from going rancid. Rosemary extract is also effective in the protection of color and flavor in natural soaps and improves the stability of natural color extracts.

Spirulina is a blue-green fresh water algae with a high vitamin, mineral, and nutrient content. It is known to have moisturizing and tightening properties when applied to the skin, as well as the antioxidant and replenishing properties from its protein-rich constitution. Spirulina creates a lovely deep green soap as the chlorophyll retains its color during saponification (many ingredients deteriorate during this process and end up brown).

St. John's wort tincture is renowned for its antidepressant qualities. St. John's wort is also known to have antibacterial and antifungal qualities when applied to the skin.

Thyme has a strong, pungent aroma which aids concentration and focus, as well as being an excellent bronchial and lung stimulant, making it valuable for treating bronchitis, coughs, colds, asthma, and the like. It has warming qualities which are great for rheumatism, sciatica, arthritis, and gout. Use fresh from the garden for extra vigor.

Turmeric (or haldi) is used in ayurvedic medicine (a preventive medical system practiced in India) where it is known as "the great cleanser." Turmeric has many valuable skin care properties such as being anti-inflammatory, antiseptic, and antibacterial. The healing properties of turmeric are now widely recognized by western researchers. In soap making this spice creates a rich golden color as well as adding its many other beneficial qualities to the soap. In India turmeric is often referred to as the "spice of life."

Vitamin E oil can be used as a skin nutrient and also as a preservative as it is an antioxidant, helping the oils in your soap to last longer before going rancid. Vitamin E protects our skin cells and allows reactive molecules to strike the cell without damaging it, protecting the skin from ultraviolet radiation. Vitamin E–rich foods, when consumed, can directly travel to the cell membranes of the skin and help to protect it. Vitamin E comes in the form of gel, capsules, and with carrier oils. Oils and gels can be applied topically to help protect the skin and are good for healing scars. The active ingredient in vitamin E is alpha-tocopherol which, in its natural form, is powdery and thick. Hence it is mixed with a carrier such as olive oil to create vitamin E oil.

Equipment

You don't need a huge amount of specialized equipment to begin making soap. In fact, you are likely to already have many of the items needed in your kitchen. However, weighing scales that weigh in one-ounce increments will make weighing your ingredients much easier. Do be careful not to use metal equipment during the soap making process unless it is enameled or stainless steel as the soap mixture is caustic and will ruin your implement or container as well as adversely affect your soap.

You will need

Heat source, such as a kitchen stove, to melt your butters and solid oils.

Medium-sized heavy pan in which to melt your butters and solid oils.

Heavy heat-proof plastic, acrylic, or wooden spoon to stir the melting butters and soap mixture.

Small heat-proof bowl or jug to put your sodium hydroxide crystals into. It must be heat-proof, as when you add the water the lye solution becomes very hot.

Large mixing bowl to put the smaller bowl in while carrying the lye solution to prevent it from spilling onto you, your floor, or surfaces (a sink bowl can be used if you don't have a big enough mixing bowl). If your bowl is made of plastic use a layer of newspaper as a barrier between the larger and smaller bowls to prevent the plastic from getting too hot and melting.

Large jug to mix all of your ingredients together in. You will be stirring the mixture vigorously so make sure the jug is big enough to allow you to do this comfortably. You could use a large bowl for this but a jug allows you to easily pour the mixture into your molds.

Small measuring jug or bowl to pour the measured water into.

Wooden or heavy plastic stick, such as a chopstick, to mix the lye solution with. A wooden stick or spoon will start to deteriorate over time through contact with the caustic solution and splinters will start to fall into your mixture, so if you are using a wooden implement be sure to replace it often.

Thermometer to measure the temperature of your mixtures—a yogurt thermometer is ideal.

Weighing scales to weigh out your ingredients. When weighing butters I would recommend lining the bowl with paper towels to prevent it from becoming greasy. When weighing liquid you may find it easier to use your plastic measuring jug rather than the bowl, but remember to weigh your jug first and zero the scale before adding the liquid.

Long, slim knife for cutting the finished soaps.

Handheld mixer to mix all of the ingredients together in the final stage. I would not recommend using this until you are confident about the soap making process as it speeds things up. Start off using a plastic or wooden spoon until you are comfortable with the trace stage (see page 59, step 8).

Trays or molds made from flexible, non-metallic materials that will allow you to easily remove the finished soaps. For the quantities given in recipes in this book a half-gallon ice-cream tub is perfect and will make eight bars each weighing approximately 3½ oz. (the bars won't weigh exactly 3½ oz. as the soap loses weight through water evaporation during curing, and the amount of evaporation varies, but this is a good guide). See page 53 for more on molds.

Wax paper, plastic-wrap, or florists' cellophane to line your soap molds. At the point when you need to remove the soap from the mold it will have a similar consistency to a block of cheese so, as you can imagine, it will be sticky and can easily adhere to the sides of the container if it is not lined.

Shelves to place the soap on while it sets and cures, in a warm room where air can circulate.

Cardboard to lightly cover and insulate your trays of fresh soap before you take them out of the molds.

Tea towel or paper towels to cover your soap when it is out of the mold and cut up, insulating it while it cures.

Gloves and goggles to protect your hands and eyes. I would recommend wearing thin rubber gloves and plastic goggles during the whole soap making process. The thin latex gloves used by chefs and dentists are good for this purpose and can be bought in boxes so you can just throw them out after you've used them (natural latex is biodegradable so you can dispose of your gloves with a clear conscience!).

Techniques

The various techniques you will need to create colors and effects in your homemade soaps are all explained here, as well as some important information on how to get the best from your ingredients. On the following pages you'll also find a few secrets that will make things a bit easier—so you don't have to learn soap making the hard way!

Making infusions

Water infusions are created by adding hot water to your ingredients and leaving to infuse overnight. You may prefer to add warm rather than hot water if you are creating an infusion from a particularly sensitive ingredient such as cucumber or oats. The longer you leave the infusion the stronger it becomes, but if you leave it for more than a couple of days it may start to ferment. Even the little alcohol produced during the initial stages of fermentation will influence the properties of the soap. For example, if calendula is left to infuse overnight the resulting infusion will create a golden opaque soap, but if left for three or four days it will begin to ferment and the tiny amount of alcohol produced will create a slightly translucent soap.

To remove any residue from the infusion, strain the liquid using a sieve or some cheesecloth. You can then use the infusion to replace some, or all, of the water in your recipe. You can make a water infusion with whatever you like—cucumber is great, as is fresh rosemary, orange, lemon, mint, or almost anything which will allow its properties to be transferred to water. You will find as you experiment with various ingredients that some infusions will affect the color of your soap and some won't. You may even find that you hit upon a wonderful new soap color!

Oil infusions are useful in soap making as some botanicals release their soluble contents into oil more easily than water. Alkanet is an example of such an ingredient and is used in the recipes in this book to create a rich lavender-colored soap (when making an alkanet infusion be sure not to leave the dry ingredient in the oil for longer than 48 hours or it may react with your soap mixture and ruin your batch). To make an oil infusion add about three tablespoons of your dry ingredient to some, or all, of the oil you will be using in your soap recipe (which will usually be olive oil as this often forms the largest proportion of liquid oil used) and leave overnight. As with water infusions the longer you leave the ingredient to infuse the stronger the color will be. Strain the infusion and use the resulting oil to replace some of the oil in your recipe.

Mixing infusions is a great way to create a particular color. When mixing infusions, the resulting color is generally what you would expect to achieve. (See pages 26–44 for specific ingredients and the colors they create in the finished soap.) For instance, mixing black tea (which produces a rich brown soap) with calendula (which produces a golden soap) produces a rich, golden brown color. When using black tea for this purpose be careful not to make your infusion too strong or it may cause the soap to set too quickly. (This quickening of the setting process is often referred to as seizing up.)

Creating effects

Marbled soaps are an attractive way to combine different ingredients. To make a marbled soap, pour ⅔ of your soap mixture into the mold and then add your colorant to the remaining ⅓ of mixture, stirring it quickly but gently. Pour this over the mixture already in the mold, using a knife or wooden spoon to quickly but carefully zigzag back and forth or swirl the knife around to create a marbled effect.

Layered soaps require two sets of molds and a double batch of soap mixture. To make a layered soap, first choose the two soap types you would like to layer. Make the first batch of soap and pour half of the mixture into each mold. Then make the second batch. By the time the second batch is ready to pour the first layer should have hardened enough to allow the second layer to sit on top rather than sinking in. Do not use milk soap to make a layered soap as milk soaps tend to shrink as they cure, which may cause your layers to come apart or warp.

Adding texture

Powders such as spirulina and turmeric add a slight gritty texture and so are great for adding color without dramatically altering the soap's texture.

Ground spices such as cinnamon will create a slightly gritty bar of soap and are great for making a gently exfoliating bar. Simply use less of the dry ingredient for a less scrubby soap.

Exfoliating ingredients such as oats, ground pumice, poppy seeds, loofah, and desiccated coconut all have different but quite pronounced exfoliating qualities. Be careful not to add too much or you might end up with a soap that feels like sandpaper!

Making milk soaps

Milk is wonderfully moisturizing and soothing, and adding milk to your soaps is a great way to harness these benefits. To make a milk soap, first chill the milk thoroughly (milk is best used when it nearly frozen so it is a good idea to freeze it and then put it in the fridge the day before so it is barely defrosted) then replace half of the total amount of water in the recipe with milk. Create the lye solution with water, being very careful when mixing as it will be twice as strong as usual since you are only using half the water. Let the lye solution cool to around body temperature (this is cooler than for other soap making), feeling the bottom of the bowl to check the temperature, then gradually add the cold milk to the solution, stirring thoroughly and carefully all of the time.

The whole process for making milk soaps should be carried out at 95°F. When the oil mixture reaches this temperature, pour your lye-milk mix into it and stir to combine thoroughly. The cooler the temperature, although not below 95°F, the lighter the soap will be, and the warmer, although never over 104°F, the darker your soap will be. If you were to make this soap at the same temperature as other soaps it would end up brown as the milk reacts with the lye solution and discolors.

You can also make milk soaps using powdered milk. First dilute the powder in water as instructed on the container and add it in the same way as fresh milk (see above). If you add it dry at the trace stage (see page 59, step 8) it may work but you could end up with rather lumpy, sour-smelling soap as the powder may stick together in dry clumps, slowly deteriorating in your soap. You can try adding powdered milk to re-milled soap, or replace some of the water needed for this process with milk (see pages 98–99).

Stamping

You can buy stamps specifically
designed for soaps (see Suppliers on
page 126), make your own, or try other
types of stamps to see if they work. One of
the easiest ways to make a stamp is to carve a
pattern, shape, or word at the end of a piece of wood measuring 1½ in.
square and 4 in. tall. Another option is to create a disc from modeling
clay (the type that goes hard when you bake it in the oven) that fits
on the end of your wooden block. Bake the disk until hard, carve
the desired shape, and stick it to your wooden block.

To create a stamp effect, place your stamp over the center
of each bar of soap and tap it reasonably hard (but not
too hard or the soap will buckle and crack) three times
using a wooden mallet or a small hammer. Then carefully
lift the stamp off and see how your imprint looks.
Sometimes the print isn't clear and this may be because
there are not enough air channels in your stamp. Make
sure your grooves are deep enough and keep adjusting
your stamp and repeating the process until you are
happy with the result.

Using molds

Flexible molds are essential as it is almost impossible to remove soap from a rigid mold due to soap's sticky consistency which causes it to adhere to the mold.

Lining molds is a good idea if you are using a plain tray mold (one that is not specific to soap making so does not have soap bar indentations). Wax paper, plastic-wrap, or florists' cellophane work well. My preference is florists' cellophane as it creates a smooth, flat surface in the soap mold and plastic-wrap can be difficult to lay flat without getting wrinkles. Measure your mold and cut two strips of your lining which are long and wide enough to cover the bottom and sides of the mold. Lay both strips across the mold, press firmly into the corners, and tape them in place on the outside of the mold.

Chilling the finished soap will make it easier to remove from the mold. If you are having trouble removing your soap, put it in the freezer for 30 minutes. Set a timer, as if you forget about it the soap can be ruined. You don't actually want to freeze your soap, but just to leave it in the cold long enough so that when you remove it from the freezer condensation forms around the soap, creating a layer of water between the soap and the mold, making the soap pop out easier. When the 30 minutes are up, have a tray ready and turn your mold upside down over the tray. Gently flex the mold and push the bottom of it gently to release the soap. Be careful not to flex or push too much or you may crack the mold, and if you are using decorative molds be careful that all of the soap is out and you don't lose some of the pattern in the mold. If it still won't come out, put it back in the freezer for another 10 minutes and try again. You will find that some molds work better than others, but it is really a matter of trial and error to see what works for you.

Making soap

What a wonderful world of soap you have entered. Here are the recipes to get you started on an adventure that will take you down a road that may change your life forever! Be warned, soap making can become very addictive—for you, your skin, and also for family and friends who will want you to make their favorite bars time and time again. Once you start making soap, you may not be allowed to stop—not that you'll want to!

The basics

The aim of this book is to make soap that your skin will reward you for using—and believe me, you'll be able to feel the difference. Each soap contains a carefully selected combination of oils, butters, essential oils, and infusions to suit a particular skin type, character, or purpose.

Take a look at the ingredients in each soap and see what fits your requirements, whether your aim is to make bath-time appealing for the kids or to soothe sensitive, irritable skin, there is a recipe here to suit. And, of course, you can create your own individual variations too. Make soap personal—after all, you are the only one who really knows what your skin likes. Your skin is your largest organ and absorbs much of what you put on it, so why not treat it well?

Basic soap recipe

The amount of soap you will make in each recipe is roughly the same and will use the same amount of water and sodium hydroxide (except in the recipes containing milk—see page 51). Each batch will produce eight $3^1/2$ oz. bars of soap, give or take a few grams, once they have cured. Of course, you can cut your soap into as many bars as you like, this is just to give you an idea of how much soap these recipes make.

The amount and variety of oils, butters, and other ingredients will vary for each recipe. However, each recipe contains palm oil, coconut oil, and olive oil in varying proportions, as I have found that this combination of oils creates a gentle soap with a firm texture and rich, silky lather. If you decide to create your own recipes you can try adding various quantities of base oils and I am sure will find your own favorite combinations. However do remember that in order to make a firm bar you should use at least 25 percent saturated fats.

Each recipe contains a different set of ingredients, but the following technique applies to all of the soap recipes with slight variations for marbled soap, layered soap, and milk soap. Where a variation occurs, the recipe will direct you to the relevant instructions.

Technique

1. Make sure you have a clean, clear surface area to work on and are not likely to be interrupted for an hour or so (probably two hours is best for your first batch). There are some very crucial time-sensitive stages in the soap making process and distractions at these points could spell the failure of your soap batch.

2. Lay out your soap molds or tray. It is best to line tray molds with wax paper, plactic-wrap, or florists' cellophane to help the soap pop out of the tray (see page 53). Be sure to fold the paper carefully at the edges and corners and secure in place with some tape on the underside, as any wrinkles will show in your finished soaps. If you are using molds which cannot easily be lined, pour the soap directly into the container and then when you want to remove it pop the molds in the freezer for 30 minutes to loosen the soap. When removed from the freezer a layer of condensation builds up between the soap and the container, allowing the soap to come out more freely.

3. Measure out your butters and oils. The butters and solid oils go into your small heavy-bottomed pan and your liquid oils can be measured directly into your large jug or mixing bowl. Prepare your added ingredients, such as essential oils, colorants, nutrients, and infusions and measure out where possible. It is a good idea to create the essential oil mix in a separate bottle ready to be poured otherwise you might start to panic when the soap is setting and you are trying to count out drops of essential oils!

4. Melt the solid oils and butters in a heavy pan over a low heat, taking care not to heat the mixture above 104°F as this will cause the oils to deteriorate. Once the solid oils and butters have nearly melted turn the heat off and allow the residual heat to melt them completely.

5. Put on your gloves and goggles. Weigh the sodium hydroxide and place into a glass, enamel, or ceramic jug or bowl. Place on a heat-proof surface in a well-ventilated area. Add the water to the sodium hydroxide crystals while stirring gently all the time. Keep your face well away from the mixture and make sure not to splash the solution while you are stirring it. Once the crystals have dissolved, leave the solution to cool until the temperature reaches between 95 and 104°F—this is the optimum temperature for making all except milk soaps.

6. Add the melted butters and oils to the liquid oils in a large jug or bowl, ensuring the temperature remains between 95 and 104°F. If the mixture gets too cold, place the bowl in a sink full of hot water and stir gently until the temperature rises. If the oils are not warm enough, return them to the pan and heat very gently until they reach the correct temperature. You should also do the same with the lye mixture.

7. Once both the lye solution and the oil mixture have reached the correct temperature, slowly pour the lye mixture into the oil, stirring all the time. The mixture needs to be stirred vigorously but carefully so you don't create any air bubbles. You can either stir by hand using a heavy spoon or use a hand-held mixer on its lowest setting. However, do take care if using an electric mixer as this can speed the process up. Be sure to reach all areas of the bowl, mixing the ingredients thoroughly using a figure-eight pattern to ensure the lye solution and the oils are thoroughly combined.

8. You now need to watch for the soap mixture to reach the trace stage. You will see that the mixture will slowly thicken as you stir, and will become the consistency of custard. When it is thick enough to leave a trace on top of the soap before sinking in when you dribble a little of the mixture into the bowl, the soap has reached the trace stage. It may take some time to reach the correct consistency—sometimes 20 minutes or more—so be patient. The trace stage is the most important point in soap making. If it cannot be reached and the mixture is not of the correct consistency, discard the mixture and begin again.

9. Once you are confident that the trace stage has been reached, quickly add any dry ingredients, essential oils, and preservative (for the recipes in this book this is grapefruit seed extract), stirring gently all the time until thoroughly combined. You need to be as quick as you can as the soap mixture

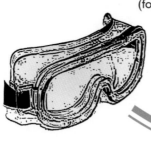

will rapidly thicken at this stage. The essential oils are added at this point to allow their scents to be carried through to the finished soaps. (When using essential oils, note that there are around 20 drops per ml, 5 ml per teaspoon and one ml is equal to around ⅕ teaspoon.) The amount of essential oils used can be varied to suit your preference, but be careful not to add too much (see Warning on page 33).

10. Pour the mixture into your molds or tray (a half-gallon ice cream tub will work well for any of the recipes given in this book). Keeping the tray level, tap it gently on the work surface to settle the mixture and encourage any air bubbles to come to the surface.

11. Cover the tray lightly with a piece of cardboard, making sure it does not touch the soap (this insulates the soap a little, helping it to saponify) and place the soap in a warm room where there is plenty of air circulation. Shelves are ideal.

12. Leave the soap for 24–48 hours, allowing it time to harden. Once the soap is hard put your gloves on and, if you lined your molds, lift your soap out of the mold. If you are using small molds or have not lined your mold, stick them in the freezer for 30 minutes (don't forget about them!). Make sure you wear gloves at any time you are likely to come into contact with the soap or the molds as the soap is still caustic at this stage as it has not finished saponifying.

13. If you are using molds, pop the soaps out onto a tray and they're ready to cure. If you need to cut your soap up, put your slab of soap onto a cutting board. Using a knife, carefully mark lines on the soap to show where it will be cut. If you wish, you can stamp a design onto your soaps at this stage (see page 52). To cut the soaps, press a long kitchen knife into the soap, carefully cutting it right through. This is harder than you might imagine as the soap is quite sticky—rather like a big slab of cheese.

14. Place your soaps on a tray, cover lightly with a tea towel or some paper towels, and put them somewhere warm and well-ventilated to cure. This process takes about a month. Before this time they have not yet fully saponified. The soap will not be firm or lather properly and it will still be slightly caustic, so it is most important to let the soaps cure fully. If you have the patience to let them cure for longer than a month they will get harder. Large temperature fluctuations can impact the curing time—cold temperatures mean that the soaps will take longer to cure while warm temperatures will speed up the process. Use your judgment to asses how the temperature in your home and the room you leave the soaps to cure in will affect the process, and adjust the curing time accordingly.

15. During curing a fine, powdery residue may appear as a thin coat on top of the soap. As long as this is just a surface residue (and not more than $1/8$ inch deep) it is harmless, but can be scraped off if desired for cosmetic purposes. If the whole soap is powdery or crumbly, there was perhaps too much lye in the soap or the ingredients were not mixed thoroughly enough, and you will have to throw that batch out as it will be too alkaline.

16. Once the curing process is complete and the soaps are hard but not crumbly, you can enjoy the fruits of your labor!

Nourish and replenish

This is a rich, mild, creamy soap with a silky soft lather. Avocado oil nourishes your skin, penetrating deep into the derma. Hemp seed oil, a real favorite of mine, is a wonderfully rich and moisturizing oil, helping to feed your skin with many great nutrients. Camomile and lavender are calming and healing, while lavender is also gently antiseptic, creating a replenishing and relaxing bathing experience.

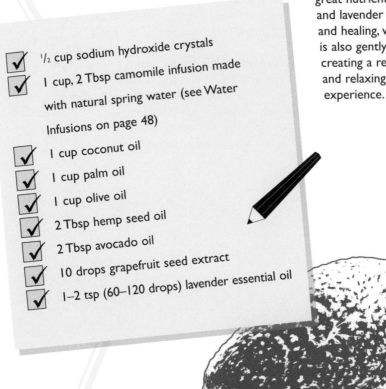

- ✓ ¹/₂ cup sodium hydroxide crystals
- ✓ I cup, 2 Tbsp camomile infusion made with natural spring water (see Water Infusions on page 48)
- ✓ I cup coconut oil
- ✓ I cup palm oil
- ✓ I cup olive oil
- ✓ 2 Tbsp hemp seed oil
- ✓ 2 Tbsp avocado oil
- ✓ 10 drops grapefruit seed extract
- ✓ I–2 tsp (60–120 drops) lavender essential oil

Pep up and invigorate

Lime and peppermint essential oils are a combination that can't fail to rejuvenate even the most sluggish minds and bodies. Peppermint makes our skin tingle and perks up our senses while lime just dives in and gives us a citrus slap!

Oatmeal is added to this soap as it is an emollient, conditioning the skin as well as providing a nice gentle scrubbiness to wake up your skin and slough away dead skin cells.

- ☑ ½ cup sodium hydroxide crystals
- ☑ 1 cup, 2 Tbsp natural spring water
- ☑ 1 cup coconut oil
- ☑ 1 cup palm oil
- ☑ 1½ cups olive oil
- ☑ 10 drops grapefruit seed extract
- ☑ ¾ tsp (45 drops) lime essential oil
- ☑ 1 tsp (60 drops) peppermint essential oil
- ☑ 1 Tbsp oatmeal (you can add more if you like it really scrubby, or less if you like it less scrubby—it's up to you!)

Sensitive soother

This soap contains no added essential oils, just lashings of moisturizing cocoa butter and light apricot seed oil (or sweet almond oil, which has very similar properties) which are easily absorbed by sensitive skin. Calming camomile infusion adds to the gentle, healing nature of this soap. Although there are no scents added, this soap has its own clean aroma—the wholesome smell of fresh, natural soap!

- ✓ ½ cup sodium hydroxide crystals
- ✓ 1 cup, 2 Tbsp camomile infusion made with natural spring water (see Water Infusions on page 48)
- ✓ 1 cup coconut oil
- ✓ ⁹⁄₁₀ cup palm oil
- ✓ ³⁄₅ cup olive oil
- ✓ ⅓ cup apricot seed oil or sweet almond oil
- ✓ ½ cup cocoa butter
- ✓ 10 drops grapefruit seed extract

Zingy green kids soap

Citrus scents are great for kids—and lime is a really zesty one. This soap is especially good if the kids tend to get a bit grumpy around bath time as the lemon and lime scents invigorate and cheer—maybe not so good for nighttime baths though as it may leave the kids too invigorated to sleep! For a sleepy bath, try one of the more calming soap recipes. Spirulina, which is a nourishing and replenishing skin food as well as a natural colorant for soap, creates a fun green bar perfect for kids. Molding this soap into monster shapes would be even more appealing, or try pressing plastic insects or other small toys (without sharp edges) into the individual soaps once they have been poured into their molds.

- ½ cup sodium hydroxide crystals
- 1 cup, 2 Tbsp natural spring water
- 1 cup coconut oil
- ⁹⁄₁₀ cup palm oil
- 1½ cups olive oil
- 10 drops grapefruit seed extract
- 1 tsp (60 drops) lemon essential oil
- ¾ tsp (45 drops) lime essential oil
- 1 Tbsp spirulina

Healing pumice

- ☑ ½ cup sodium hydroxide crystals
- ☑ 1 cup, 2 Tbsp natural spring water
- ☑ 1 cup coconut oil
- ☑ 9/10 cup palm oil
- ☑ 1 cup olive oil
- ☑ 2⅖ Tbsp hemp seed oil
- ☑ 2⅖ Tbsp thistle (safflower) oil
- ☑ 1½ Tbsp neem oil
- ☑ 10 drops grapefruit seed extract
- ☑ 1 tsp (60 drops) peppermint essential oil
- ☑ ⅓ tsp (20 drops) thyme essential oil
- ☑ ⅓ tsp (20 drops) lavender essential oil
- ☑ ⅓ tsp (20 drops) rosemary essential oil
- ☑ 1 Tbsp chopped fresh garden herbs
- ☑ 1 tsp ground pumice

Thistle (safflower) oil is light, emollient, super moisturizing, and works wonderfully in salad dressing as well as a nourisher for the skin. Finely ground pumice is added to the soap base to give the soap a slightly exfoliating quality, helping to remove ground-in dirt, grease, and even tree sap (it works, honest!). In keeping with the outdoor theme, essential oils of thyme, rosemary, peppermint, and lavender are added to make a fresh bar with neem oil's antiseptic properties to help heal any cuts and abrasions.

You can replace pumice with the same amount of semolina or cornmeal for a rounder abrasion, or try a teaspoon of each for a really scrubby soap!

Hippy heaven

The mixture of black tea and calendula petal infusion creates a lovely, rich, caramel-colored bar. With lashings of patchouli essential oil, this soap gives you and your bathroom a distinctly woody, eastern aroma reminiscent of the 1960s. There is also a lot of hemp seed oil which was very popular during the hippy era. So here's a little something for all you old hippies out there, and all the new ones too!

- ☑ ½ cup sodium hydroxide crystals
- ☑ 1 cup, 2 Tbsp black tea and calendula infusion made with natural spring water (made using one tea bag and a handful of calendula petals—see Water Infusions on page 48)
- ☑ 1 cup coconut oil
- ☑ ⁹⁄₁₀ cup palm oil
- ☑ 1¼ cup olive oil
- ☑ 1¼ cup hemp seed oil
- ☑ 10 drops grapefruit seed extract
- ☑ 1–2 tsp (60–120 drops) patchouli essential oil

Pamper and indulge

Hemp seed oil creates a particularly rich, smooth, and luxurious lather to really pamper skin in need of a treat. With a rich golden color and pretty bright gold petals scattered throughout, this soap looks good just sitting in the soap dish. Jasmine and sandalwood are classic eastern aphrodisiac and skin-nurturing essential oils, while ylang ylang creates a heady, sensuous aroma that lingers on the skin. Indulgent and aromatic, this soap is a must-have for those "me-time" candle-lit baths.

- [x] ½ cup sodium hydroxide crystals
- [x] 1 cup, 2 Tbsp calendula infusion made with natural spring water (see Water Infusions on page 48)
- [x] 1 cup coconut oil
- [x] ⁹/₁₀ cup palm oil
- [x] 1¼ cups olive oil
- [x] ¼ cup hemp seed oil
- [x] 10 drops grapefruit seed extract
- [x] ¾ tsp (45 drops) ylang ylang essential oil
- [x] ¾ tsp (45 drops) jasmine essential oil
- [x] ½ tsp (30 drops) sandalwood essential oil
- [x] 1 small handful calendula petals

Relax and de-stress

This soap starts out with a rather dull, dark hue and you can watch it develop its purple color as it saponifies. Lavender buds speckle this pretty purple soap, and the alkanet infusion (which gives the soap its color) conditions the skin. Lavender essential oil is both healing and relaxing, while clary sage performs the task of putting your mind at ease with its soporific qualities. I would recommend using this soap to relax in the evening rather than before a busy day.

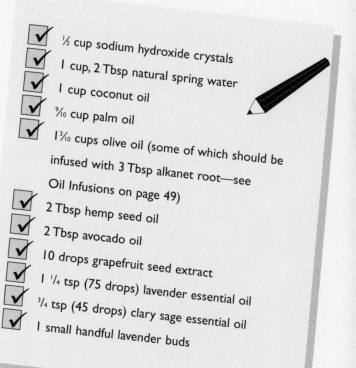

- ½ cup sodium hydroxide crystals
- I cup, 2 Tbsp natural spring water
- I cup coconut oil
- ⁹/₁₀ cup palm oil
- I³/₁₀ cups olive oil (some of which should be infused with 3 Tbsp alkanet root—see Oil Infusions on page 49)
- 2 Tbsp hemp seed oil
- 2 Tbsp avocado oil
- 10 drops grapefruit seed extract
- I ¼ tsp (75 drops) lavender essential oil
- ³/₄ tsp (45 drops) clary sage essential oil
- I small handful lavender buds

Marbled detox

This soap is made in two stages: the first, creating the white portion, and the second, swirling green through it. Full instructions for creating a marbled soap are given on page 50. Green tea and grapefruit seed extract provide an antioxidant mix to draw impurities from your skin, while spirulina gives the green bit its vibrant color and feeds your skin all the good things it's missing. Neroli and bergamot essential oils create an uplifting and soothing blend to detox the mind as well as the body!

- ½ cup sodium hydroxide crystals
- 1 cup, 2 Tbsp green tea infusion made with natural spring water (use one tea bag—see Water Infusions on page 48)
- 1 cup coconut oil
- 9/10 cup palm oil
- 1½ cups olive oil
- 20 drops grapefruit seed extract
- 1 ¼ tsp (75 drops) bergamot essential oil
- ¾ tsp (45 drops) neroli essential oil
- 1 Tbsp spirulina for the marbling (add only to the final ⅓ of the mixture)

Winter warmer

This is a soap perfect for cold winter mornings and crisp autumn evenings. It will warm your senses with its citrus and spice and nourish cold, chapped skin with lashings of healing hemp seed oil and rich cocoa butter. Cinnamon is a warming oil and ground turmeric, renowned in India for its beneficial properties for the skin, gives this soap a rich russet tinge. Cinnamon helps keep colds and flu at bay, vitamin C–rich orange essential oil boosts your skin's defenses and the cheerful scent keeps those winter blues at bay.

✓ ½ cup sodium hydroxide crystals
✓ 1 cup, 2 Tbsp natural spring water
✓ 1 cup coconut oil
✓ ⁹⁄₁₀ cup palm oil
✓ 1 cup olive oil
✓ ⅓ cup cocoa butter
✓ 1½ Tbsp hemp seed oil
✓ 10 drops grapefruit seed extract
✓ 1 tsp (60 drops) sweet orange essential oil
✓ ½ tsp (30 drops) cinnamon essential oil
✓ ½ tsp (30 drops) nutmeg essential oil
✓ 1 tsp ground turmeric

Silky shampoo

- ½ cup sodium hydroxide crystals
- 1 cup, 2 Tbsp natural spring water
- ⅔ cup coconut oil
- 6⅓ Tbsp palm oil
- 2½ cups olive oil
- ¼ cup castor oil
- 1 tsp neem oil
- 10 drops grapefruit seed extract
- 1 tsp (60 drops) peppermint essential oil
- ½ tsp (30 drops) rosemary essential oil
- ½ tsp (30 drops) eucalyptus essential oil

Shampoo in a bar is a very popular and practical choice as it can also be used as an all-over cleansing bar. The castor oil in this soap is great for retaining moisture in the hair and scalp, and regular use can help to alleviate dandruff. This bar conditions as well as cleans, creating a rich, creamy lather scented with invigorating peppermint to get your scalp tingling, rosemary to make hair shiny and smooth, and eucalyptus to wake up those brain cells!

Clean shave

Before you begin to create this soap, it is worth noting that it will take six weeks to cure due to the kaolin. This traditional shaving soap made with a small amount of natural kaolin clay allows your razor to glide a few microns away from your skin. This gives a gentler shave as the blade doesn't come into contact with the skin and so won't cause irritation. I would suggest putting a chunk of this into a shaving dish or enameled tin so you can lather it up properly before applying to the face, legs, under-arms, or wherever else you are planning to shave! Neem oil and camomile are used for their healing qualities, and olive oil conditions the skin. Bergamot is a powerful antidepressant as well as having antibacterial properties while sandalwood cares for the skin and grounds the senses, and juniper's astringent, toning qualities leave your skin radiant.

- ☑ ½ cup sodium hydroxide crystals
- ☑ 1 cup, 2 Tbsp camomile infusion made with natural spring water (see Water Infusions on page 48)
- ☑ 1 cup coconut oil
- ☑ 1 cup palm oil
- ☑ 1¹/₁₀ cups olive oil
- ☑ 1¹/₅ tsp neem oil
- ☑ 10 drops grapefruit seed extract
- ☑ ³/₄ tsp (45 drops) bergamot essential oil
- ☑ ³/₄ tsp (45 drops) sandalwood essential oil
- ☑ ¹/₂ tsp (30 drops) juniper essential oil
- ☑ 1 tsp kaolin

Oat, honey, and hemp face soap

If you like to wash your face with soap, you should treat it a little bit gentler than the rest of your skin as your facial skin is more delicate. This soap is gentle and caring and will leave your face soft and silky smooth—no guarantees about less wrinkles though! Hemp seed oil nourishes, moisturizes, and feeds your skin the nutrients it may have lost during the course of the day. Oats are an emollient and also provide a very gentle exfoliating quality. Honey is naturally antibacterial and healing, as well as conditioning to the skin and helps to create a lovely, soft creamy bar of soap. No essential oils are used as the subtle scent of honey, oats, and fresh soap are enough and you don't want to over-burden sensitive facial skin when what we really want is to help it get rid of residues and toxins in the most efficient, caring way possible—without any unnecessary additives.

- ☑ $1/2$ cup sodium hydroxide crystals
- ☑ 1 cup, 2 Tbsp natural spring water
- ☑ 1 cup coconut oil
- ☑ $9/10$ cup palm oil
- ☑ $1 1/4$ cups olive oil
- ☑ $1/4$ cup hemp seed oil
- ☑ 10 drops grapefruit seed extract
- ☑ 1 Tbsp honey
- ☑ 1 Tbsp rolled oats

Rough and ready

See page 50 for instructions on making marbled soaps. This soap is for those of you who like to give your skin a good scrub once in a while. The poppy seeds act as little exfoliating balls, rubbing against the skin and helping to slough away dead skin cells. Turmeric is known in the East as a skin healer, and when used in soap it creates a lovely golden color. Cocoa butter creates a firm bar with ultra-moisturizing qualities, while the hemp seed oil nourishes your skin. Mandarin essential oil is one of my favorites with its fresh, vital scent and stress-relieving properties, and ginger is warming both in aroma and to the touch.

- ✓ $\frac{1}{2}$ cup sodium hydroxide crystals
- ✓ 1 cup, 2 Tbsp natural spring water
- ✓ 1 cup coconut oil
- ✓ $\frac{9}{10}$ cup palm oil
- ✓ 1 cup olive oil
- ✓ $\frac{1}{3}$ cocoa butter
- ✓ 1 $\frac{1}{2}$ Tbsp hemp seed oil
- ✓ 10 drops grapefruit seed extract
- ✓ 1 $\frac{1}{4}$ tsp (75 drops) mandarin essential oil
- ✓ $\frac{3}{4}$ tsp (45 drops) ginger essential oil
- ✓ 1 Tbsp poppy seeds
- ✓ 1 Tbsp turmeric (added to the last $\frac{1}{3}$ of the mix, for marbling)

Creamy Cleopatra

Queen Cleopatra could afford the best, and in her time the best skin care was apparently ass' milk. Well, today we can afford the best too but will settle for good old cows' milk instead of searching out an ass to milk. Or you can use goats' milk if you prefer. The milk nourishes deep into the derma, soothing any external irritations. The scent of neroli is a reputed aphrodisiac in some countries, and I think one of the most delicious scent combinations is light, bright, heady neroli and skin conditioning, earthy sandalwood. A real Eastern treat fit for a queen!

- ✓ ¹/₂ cup sodium hydroxide crystals
- ✓ ¹/₂ cup, 1 Tbsp natural spring water
- ✓ ¹/₂ cup, 1 Tbsp milk (well chilled—see page 51 for instructions on making milk soaps)
- ✓ ⁶/₇ cup coconut oil
- ✓ ³/₄ cup palm oil
- ✓ 1⁵/₆ cups olive oil
- ✓ 1¹/₂ cups castor oil
- ✓ 1²/₅ cups cocoa butter
- ✓ 10 drops grapefruit seed extract
- ✓ 1 ¹/₄ tsp (75 drops) neroli essential oil
- ✓ ³/₄ tsp (45 drops) sandalwood essential oil
- ✓ Small handful calendula petals

Tea tree healer

Whether it's for athlete's foot or spotty, teenage skin, this soap will help bring those unfriendly bacteria under control. Tea tree gets right in there among those naughty alien bacteria, helping your natural bacteria gain the lead, while eucalyptus and mint wake up your skin and your mind. Spirulina feeds some of the good things back to your skin to give it the weapons it needs to keep those invading bacteria at bay in the future, as well as making this soap a gorgeous rich green color. As tea tree is a very strong oil, it is a good idea to do a patch test before using the soap on your whole face to make sure your skin can handle it.

☑ ½ cup sodium hydroxide crystals

☑ I cup, 2 Tbsp natural spring water

☑ I cup coconut oil

☑ ⁹/₁₀ cup palm oil

☑ I½ cups olive oil

☑ 10 drops grapefruit seed extract

☑ ⅓ tsp (20 drops) tea tree essential oil

☑ ⅓ tsp (20 drops) peppermint essential oil

☑ 10 drops eucalyptus essential oil

☑ I Tbsp spirulina

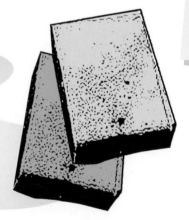

Fisherman's aniseed

Aniseed is well known in the fishing world for attracting fish and masking odors, so is helpful at disguising our own smell when handling bait and tackle. While this soap will be a real hit with fishing enthusiasts out there, it is also is a great day-to-day soap as it helps deodorize all sorts of smells. The hint of peppermint in this soap combined with fresh and spicy aniseed is all you'll need to set you up for a hard day on the riverbank—or a hard day anywhere else for that matter. And it might just help keep those nasty flies and mosquitoes away as well! The combination of black tea and alkanet infusion in this recipe give a rich deep color to this useful bar.

- [x] $1/2$ cup sodium hydroxide crystals
- [x] 1 cup, 2 Tbsp black tea infusion made with natural spring water (see Water Infusions on page 48)
- [x] 1 cup coconut oil
- [x] $9/10$ cup palm oil
- [x] $3/5$ cup olive oil (infused with 1 Tbsp alkanet root—see Oil Infusions on page 49)
- [x] $1/3$ cup apricot seed oil or sweet almond oil
- [x] $1/2$ cup cocoa butter
- [x] 10 drops grapefruit seed extract
- [x] $3/4$ tsp (45 drops) aniseed essential oil
- [x] $3/4$ tsp (45 drops) peppermint essential oil

Earl grey

Bergamot stimulates the mind and aids concentration, and there's nothing like a nice cup of earl grey tea to get you feeling back on track. So this soap has been created along a similar theme, but instead of drinking it, you're washing with it. Good in the morning to get you going for a day at the office or perhaps to help you with your studying, but also good before a night out to heighten your senses and help you to carry on for longer. A green-tea infusion is used to help detox the system and to give a little more tea to this tea-themed soap, without the dark color of black tea.

- [x] ½ cup sodium hydroxide crystals
- [x] 1 cup, 2 Tbsp green tea infusion made with natural spring water (see Water Infusions on page 48)
- [x] 1 cup coconut oil
- [x] ⁹⁄₁₀ cup palm oil
- [x] 1½ cups olive oil
- [x] 10 drops grapefruit seed extract
- [x] 1–2 tsp (60–120 drops) bergamot essential oil

Nutritious and delicious

See page 50 for instructions on making a layered soap. This soap has a pretty, two-tone layer effect, with yellow lemon soap on top and green lime soap on the bottom. The top layer is made using a calendula infusion to give a bright, rich yellow glow, as well as nourishing hemp seed oil and invigorating lemon essential oil. The second layer feeds the skin yet more of the good stuff as it's packed with spirulina, giving it a healthy deep green hue, as well as zingy lime essential oil to complete this citrus combo.

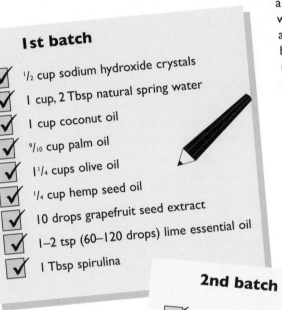

1st batch

- ✓ ¹/₂ cup sodium hydroxide crystals
- ✓ 1 cup, 2 Tbsp natural spring water
- ✓ 1 cup coconut oil
- ✓ ⁹/₁₀ cup palm oil
- ✓ 1¹/₄ cups olive oil
- ✓ ¹/₄ cup hemp seed oil
- ✓ 10 drops grapefruit seed extract
- ✓ 1–2 tsp (60–120 drops) lime essential oil
- ✓ 1 Tbsp spirulina

2nd batch

- ✓ ¹/₂ cup sodium hydroxide crystals
- ✓ 1 cup, 2 Tbsp calendula infusion made with natural spring water (see Water Infusions on page 48)
- ✓ 1 cup coconut oil
- ✓ ⁹/₁₀ cup palm oil
- ✓ 1¹/₄ cups olive oil
- ✓ ¹/₄ cup hemp seed oil
- ✓ 10 drops grapefruit seed extract
- ✓ 1–2 tsp (60–120 drops) lemon essential oil

Truly madly deeply

This soap is a heady mix of woody, spicy scents. Cinnamon essential oil warms the skin while ground cinnamon gives the soap a light russet, speckled effect and is slightly exfoliating, boosting skin circulation. Frankincense essential oil and cocoa butter condition the skin. Hemp seed oil nourishes and conditions while cedarwood, mixed with the deep and spicy scents of frankincense and cinnamon, creates a rich, woody aroma.

- ½ cup sodium hydroxide crystals
- 1 cup, 2 Tbsp natural spring water
- 1 cup coconut oil
- ⁹/₁₀ cup palm oil
- 1¼ cups olive oil
- ⅓ cup cocoa butter
- 1½ Tbsp hemp seed oil
- 10 drops grapefruit seed extract
- ¾ tsp (45 drops) cinnamon essential oil
- ¾ tsp (45 drops) cedarwood essential oil
- ½ tsp (60 drops) frankincense essential oil
- 1 tsp ground cinnamon

Breathe deeply

- ½ cup sodium hydroxide crystals
- 1 cup, 2 Tbsp natural spring water
- 1 cup coconut oil
- ⁹/₁₀ cup palm oil
- 1½ cups olive oil
- 10 drops grapefruit seed extract
- 1 tsp (60 drops) eucalyptus essential oil
- ½ tsp (30 drops) thyme essential oil
- ½ tsp (30 drops) clary sage essential oil
- 1 Tbsp spirulina

When you're feeling a bit blocked up, take a long hot bath with this soap and breathe deeply as the eucalyptus-infused steam fills your lungs, helping to open up all those little alveoli (tiny air sacks in the lungs). A heavy dose of eucalyptus helps clear the sinuses while thyme kills those naughty bacteria that are attacking your immune system, and clary sage allows aching muscles to relax and aching minds to slow down. Best for an evening bath.

Beardy weirdy

This is a soap designed to make you smile. Beardy weirdy is a term I love, and it makes me smile whenever I hear it. So I wanted to christen this soap with that name for all those beardy weirdies out there who need some special-care soap to keep their beards happy. This soap has honey, which is naturally healing and antibacterial, as well as hemp seed oil to condition hair and skin, and both lemon and lemongrass essential oils to wake up that face and make it smile.

- ☑ ½ cup sodium hydroxide crystals
- ☑ 1 cup, 2 Tbsp natural spring water
- ☑ 1 cup coconut oil
- ☑ ⁹⁄₁₀ cup palm oil
- ☑ 1⅓ cups olive oil (some of which should be infused with 3 Tbsp alkanet root—see Oil Infusions on page 49)
- ☑ 2 Tbsp hemp seed oil
- ☑ 2 Tbsp avocado oil
- ☑ 10 drops grapefruit seed extract
- ☑ 25 drops lemon essential oil
- ☑ 25 drops lemongrass essential oil
- ☑ 2 Tbsp honey

Chocoholic

See page 50 for instructions on making a marbled soap. This rich, luxurious, and indulgent chocoholic's soap contains nourishing cocoa butter for a really firm, long-lasting bar that has tons of thick moisturizing lathery suds, castor oil to draw moisture to the skin, and cocoa powder for the final chocolate touch with heavy, dark brown swirls through the velvety, creamy soap. Vanilla and nutmeg combine to add to the divine chocolatey scent (and vanilla was also used in days gone by as an aphrodisiac). It has been reported that chocolate smells can fulfill the body's desire to eat chocolate—so you never know, this indulgent soap may even help keep you in shape!

- ☑ $^1/_2$ cup sodium hydroxide crystals
- ☑ $^1/_2$ cup, I Tbsp natural spring water
- ☑ $^1/_2$ cup, I Tbsp milk (well chilled—see page 51 for instructions on making milk soaps)
- ☑ $^6/_7$ cup coconut oil
- ☑ $^3/_4$ cup palm oil
- ☑ $1^5/_6$ cups olive oil
- ☑ $1^1/_2$ Tbsp castor oil
- ☑ $1^2/_5$ Tbsp cocoa butter
- ☑ 10 drops grapefruit seed extract
- ☑ $1^1/_4$ tsp (75 drops) vanilla essential oil or $^1/_3$ of that amount if you are using vanilla absolute
- ☑ $^3/_4$ tsp (45 drops) nutmeg essential oil
- ☑ I Tbsp cocoa powder (only added to the last $^1/_3$ of the mix for marbling)

Cool as a cucumber

This is a lovely, fresh soap that has a gentle conditioning effect on the skin and looks sort of like pieces of cucumber, if you use a bit of imagination! Hemp seed oil feeds the epidermis while avocado oil moisturizes right to the core of your skin. Cucumber is known for its gentle skin-calming qualities while mint uplifts the senses. Peppermint and bergamot essential oils invigorate the mind. At the trace stage, after adding your essential oils, quickly spoon about ¾ of the soap mix into a separate bowl. Add the spirulina to the rest of the mix and pour into your molds. Quickly get your bowl of pale soap, and spoon a dollop of this lighter soap roughly into the center of where each bar of soap will be when you cut it. This works best if you can find circular molds as then the effect is of a green skin around a creamy-colored cucumber center.

☑ ½ cup sodium hydroxide crystals

☑ I cup, 2 Tbsp fresh cucumber and mint infusion made with natural spring water (see Water Infusions on page 48)

☑ I cup coconut oil

☑ ⁹⁄₁₀ cup palm oil

☑ I ⅓ cups olive oil

☑ 2 Tbsp hemp seed oil

☑ 2 Tbsp avocado oil

☑ 10 drops grapefruit seed extract

☑ I tsp (60 drops) peppermint essential oil

☑ ½ tsp (30 drops) bergamot essential oil

☑ ½ tsp (30 drops) geranium essential oil

☑ I Tbsp spirulina (only for ¾ of the mix)

Fruity all over

This is a similar recipe to the shampoo bar on page 72 and is great for your hair as well as cleansing and nourishing your skin all over. The high percentage of castor oil draws moisture to your skin, scalp, and hair and olive oil nourishes and conditions your whole body. Neem oil is healing so will deal with anything that might need to be healed, be it a minor skin condition, scratches, or insect bites. Calendula infusion and alkanet root give this soap a soft green color while the fruity essential oils of mandarin and pink grapefruit enliven and cheer.

- ✓ $^1/_2$ cup sodium hydroxide crystals
- ✓ I cup, 2 Tbsp calendula infusion made with natural spring water (see Water Infusions on page 48)
- ✓ $^2/_3$ cup coconut oil
- ✓ $6^1/_5$ Tbsp palm oil
- ✓ $2^1/_2$ cups olive oil infused with alkanet root (use 3 Tbsp alkanet root—see Oil Infusions on page 49)
- ✓ $^1/_4$ cup castor oil
- ✓ I tsp neem oil
- ✓ 10 drops grapefruit seed extract
- ✓ I tsp (60 drops) mandarin essential oil
- ✓ I tsp (60 drops) pink grapefruit essential oil

Milk and honey

This traditional recipe combines the conditioning elements of fresh, creamy milk with the healing and antibiotic qualities of honey. If possible, find some locally produced honey as exposure to local pollen may help with allergies such as hayfever. For the full benefits eat some of the honey as well as using it in your soap. Jasmine and neroli create an intoxicating sweet and sensuous aroma, and lavender buds provide a pretty, purple-spotted effect through the creamy colored soap.

- ☑ $\frac{1}{2}$ cup sodium hydroxide crystals
- ☑ $\frac{1}{2}$ cup, 1 Tbsp natural spring water
- ☑ $\frac{1}{2}$ cup, 1 Tbsp milk, well chilled (see Milk Soaps on page 51)
- ☑ $\frac{6}{7}$ cup coconut oil
- ☑ $\frac{3}{4}$ cup palm oil
- ☑ $1\frac{5}{6}$ cups olive oil
- ☑ $1\frac{1}{2}$ Tbsp castor oil
- ☑ $1\frac{2}{5}$ Tbsp cocoa butter
- ☑ 10 drops grapefruit seed extract
- ☑ $\frac{3}{4}$ tsp (45 drops) jasmine essential oil
- ☑ 1 tsp (60 drops) neroli essential oil
- ☑ 1 Tbsp honey
- ☑ Small handful lavender buds

Wild and woody

For a bathroom full of aromatic steamy suds and scents to remind you of shady forest glades and misty woodland walks, this lovely earthy recipe is just the ticket. This soap has our trusty friend, olive oil, to create a gentle oil-rich lather, and also contains hemp seed oil to nourish and condition the skin. Grounding and clarifying patchouli, uplifting sandalwood, and circulation-boosting cedarwood make this a soap for all occasions.

- ☑ ¹/₂ cup sodium hydroxide crystals
- ☑ 1 cup, 2 Tbsp black tea infusion made with natural spring water (use one tea bag—see Water Infusions on page 48)
- ☑ 1 cup coconut oil
- ☑ ⁹/₁₀ cup palm oil
- ☑ 1¹/₄ cups olive oil
- ☑ ¹/₄ cup hemp seed oil
- ☑ 10 drops grapefruit seed extract
- ☑ 1 tsp (60 drops) sandalwood essential oil
- ☑ ¹/₂ tsp (30 drops) cedarwood essential oil
- ☑ ¹/₂ tsp (30 drops) patchouli essential oil

Fields of flowers

With everything flowery, this soap uses replenishing thistle oil—and even thistles have nice flowers! A heady mix of floral scents combine with some really nourishing base oils. Neem oil, known in the East for its healing properties, is mixed with hemp seed oil to nourish and condition the skin. Deep and sensuous ylang ylang combines with the lighter, heady aroma of jasmine, a floral aphrodisiac, and an even lighter, note of neroli to take you away to far-off places where wild flowers bloom, even in the depths of winter.

☑ ¹/₂ cup sodium hydroxide crystals
☑ 1 cup, 2 Tbsp natural spring water
☑ 1 cup coconut oil
☑ ⁹/₁₀ cup palm oil
☑ ¹/₅ cup olive oil
☑ 2 ⁴/₅ Tbsp hemp seed oil
☑ 2 ⁴/₅ Tbsp thistle (safflower) oil
☑ 1 ¹/₂ Tbsp neem oil
☑ 10 drops grapefruit seed extract
☑ ³/₄ tsp (45 drops) ylang ylang essential oil
☑ ³/₄ tsp (45 drops) neroli essential oil
☑ ¹/₂ tsp (30 drops) jasmine essential oil
☑ 1 small handful calendula petals

Tangerine dream

A little burst of color on those gray and bleary winter mornings. This is a great soap to jump into the shower and wash away those Monday morning blues with Avocado oil gives your skin some breakfast while olive oil replenishes and moisturizes. The fresh, zesty scents of tangerine, mandarin, and sweet orange enliven the mind and brighten the senses, putting a smile on your face and setting you up for the day.

- ☑ ½ cup sodium hydroxide crystals
- ☑ 1 cup, 2 Tbsp natural spring water
- ☑ 1 cup coconut oil
- ☑ ⁹/₁₀ cup palm oil
- ☑ 1⁵/₆ cups olive oil
- ☑ ¼ cup avocado oil
- ☑ 10 drops grapefruit seed extract
- ☑ ¾ tsp (45 drops) tangerine essential oil
- ☑ ¾ tsp (45 drops) mandarin essential oil
- ☑ ½ tsp (30 drops) sweet orange essential oil
- ☑ 1 Tbsp ground turmeric

Citrus burst

This zesty number is a great cellulite buster as citrus oils are known to aid circulation. Rub yourself all over, focusing on those annoying parts where cellulite accumulates, with this skin-tingling soap. As well as gently massaging this soap onto your skin, when the area is lathered up, take small portions of skin between your finger and thumb, hold firmly, and gently pinch and twist, repeating all around the affected area. Doing this regularly can help disperse cellulite build-up, allowing the fat cells to be broken down, carried away, and disposed of.

- ✓ ¹/₂ cup sodium hydroxide crystals
- ✓ I cup, 2 Tbsp natural spring water
- ✓ I cup coconut oil
- ✓ ⁹/₁₀ cup palm oil
- ✓ I cup olive oil
- ✓ ¹/₃ cup cocoa butter
- ✓ I ¹/₂ Tbsp hemp seed oil
- ✓ 10 drops grapefruit seed extract
- ✓ ³/₄ tsp (45 drops) lemon essential oil
- ✓ ³/₄ tsp (45 drops) grapefruit essential oil
- ✓ ¹/₂ tsp (30 drops) sweet orange essential oil

Go nuts

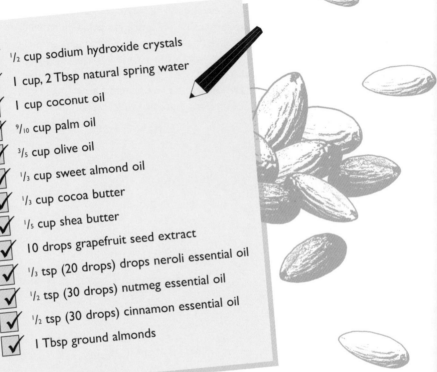

- ☑ ½ cup sodium hydroxide crystals
- ☑ 1 cup, 2 Tbsp natural spring water
- ☑ 1 cup coconut oil
- ☑ ⁹/₁₀ cup palm oil
- ☑ ³/₅ cup olive oil
- ☑ ⅓ cup sweet almond oil
- ☑ ⅓ cup cocoa butter
- ☑ ⅕ cup shea butter
- ☑ 10 drops grapefruit seed extract
- ☑ ⅓ tsp (20 drops) drops neroli essential oil
- ☑ ½ tsp (30 drops) nutmeg essential oil
- ☑ ½ tsp (30 drops) cinnamon essential oil
- ☑ 1 Tbsp ground almonds

This soap is hard and long-lasting due to the large quantity of cocoa butter. With lashings of rich shea butter to condition the skin and light, emollient sweet almond oil, this soap is packed with nutty goodness. To add that extra bit of nut value are some ground almonds, giving this soap a very gentle exfoliating quality. The scents of neroli, cinnamon, and nutmeg create a sweet, spicy aroma which makes this soap a real pleasure to use.

Hot 'n' spicy

This soap is designed to warm up tired and aching muscles and soothe the body and mind after a hard day's work. The black tea infusion gives the soap a rich, dark color while feeding the skin with natural antioxidants. Cocoa butter conditions the skin and creates a firm, long lasting bar, and hemp seed oil provides nutrients which the epidermis may be lacking. The blend of essential oils is chosen to caress and soothe—cinnamon is warming and an anti-rheumatic, ginger adds heat and helps clean out the lungs, clove lifts the mind and helps ease any chesty conditions, and clary sage is a soporific, calming both mind and muscles. Ground cinnamon adds to the spicy warming qualities and provides very gentle exfoliation.

- ½ cup sodium hydroxide crystals
- 1 cup, 2 Tbsp black tea infusion made with natural spring water (see Water Infusions on page 48)
- 1 cup coconut oil
- ⁹⁄₁₀ cup palm oil
- 1 cup olive oil
- ⅓ cocoa butter
- 1½ Tbsp hemp seed oil
- 10 drops grapefruit seed extract
- 1 tsp (45 drops) cinnamon essential oil
- ⅓ tsp (20 drops) ginger essential oil
- ⅓ tsp (20 drops) clove essential oil
- ⅓ tsp (20 drops) clary sage essential oil
- 1 tsp ground cinnamon

Honeycomb delight

This fun soap has a layer of natural beeswax at the bottom. Try to get hold of the thin honeycomb-printed beeswax layers used by candle makers and lay a sheet on the bottom of your tray mold. This looks great when it's finished, with a pretty golden honeycomb layer on top of a light, creamy honey soap. The honeycomb is also good to help scrub stubborn grime off hands or as a gentle exfoliator. Avocado oil makes this a really skin nourishing soap while honey adds a replenishing and gently healing quality. I like to leave this soap unscented as the beeswax and honey give a light, honey aroma all by themselves.

- [x] $^1/_2$ cup sodium hydroxide crystals
- [x] I cup, 2 Tbsp natural spring water
- [x] I cup coconut oil
- [x] $^9/_{10}$ cup palm oil
- [x] $1^5/_6$ cups olive oil
- [x] $^1/_4$ cup avocado oil
- [x] 20 drops grapefruit seed extract
- [x] I Tbsp honey
- [x] Thin layer of natural honeycomb-printed beeswax

Dog soap

Dogs' skin is very sensitive and in the wild wouldn't come into contact with soap. So when washing your dog try to wash just the fur and avoid rubbing soap into the skin as you may irritate it. Dogs' skin has a higher pH than ours and so is more alkaline. This recipe is great for dogs' skin and coat as it too is slightly alkaline. The castor oil in this recipe helps retain moisture in the fur and also the skin, acting like a conditioner. Citronella essential oil helps repel bugs with its pungent aroma, while tea tree is antiseptic and antibacterial. Thyme also has antibacterial qualities and lavender is soothing and healing and gives a light scent so your dog will smell great as well as be bug-free, shiny, and soft!

- ✔ $\frac{1}{2}$ cup sodium hydroxide crystals
- ✔ 1 cup, 2 Tbsp natural spring water
- ✔ 1 cup coconut oil
- ✔ $\frac{9}{10}$ cup palm oil
- ✔ 1$\frac{1}{2}$ cups olive oil
- ✔ 1$\frac{1}{2}$ Tbsp castor oil
- ✔ 10 drops grapefruit seed extract
- ✔ 1 tsp (60 drops) citronella essential oil
- ✔ $\frac{1}{3}$ tsp (20 drops) thyme essential oil
- ✔ $\frac{1}{3}$ tsp (20 drops) lavender essential oil
- ✔ $\frac{1}{3}$ tsp (20 drops) tea tree essential oil

Did you know...
...that a dog's skin pH is one of the highest (so most alkaline) among mammals, at an average of 7.4? Human skin averages a pH of 5.5 and pH 7 is neutral.

Taking soap further

Whether you have plenty of time to create a wonderful soap or need a practical bar in a hurry, there is something for every occasion in the world of soap. From quick and easy melt-and-pour soaps to whipped soap, translucent, or liquid soaps you can get as carried away or as back-to-basics as you like. In this chapter there are a few ideas to get you started. If you like a particular method or type of soap, you might like to try researching that area further.

Alternative soap making methods

Making soap from scratch is very rewarding, but there are other ways of creating luxurious soaps at home. Below are some great ideas for alternative soap-making methods.

Re-milling

You can re-mill your own soap scraps, buy ready-made soap and re-mill it, or make a batch of plain soap and re-mill it, adding your favorite fragrance. The measurements don't have to be as precise as when you are making soap from scratch.

Equipment
Grater
Large saucepan (half filled with boiling water)
Heat-proof jug
Heavy wooden or plastic spoon
Molds
Knife
Thermometer (optional)
Gloves (if you will be shaping the soaps by hand)

Ingredients
6 oz grated soap
4 Tbsp coconut oil
4 Tbsp water
½ tsp (20 drops) essential oils of your choice (see pages 33–37)
Any dry ingredients you want (see pages 40–44)

Method

1. Grate the soap and set aside.

2. Half fill your large saucepan with boiling water. Pour the grated soap, measured water, and coconut oil into the heat-proof jug and place the jug in your saucepan with the boiling water. Be very careful not to heat the mixture above 104°F— you might like to use a thermometer to check this.

3. Stir the mixture gently using the wooden or plastic spoon for 15–20 minutes, taking care not to create too many suds. Squash any lumps that appear with the back of the spoon. The mixture will start to resemble cottage cheese before becoming thick and stringy, but do be patient as this may take some time.

4. When the soap has reached the smooth, stringy, thick stage, remove from the heat and stir in your essential oils and dry ingredients.

5. Pour the mixture into molds when cooled or shape with your hands. If you are handling the soap at this stage, it is a good idea to wear protective gloves.

6. The soap should solidify in about four to five days and can then be cut and left to dry for a few weeks on well-ventilated shelves in a warm room.

Melt and pour

This method refers to ready-made soap bases which can be bought from specialist suppliers. These are simple to use and don't need time to cure, but of course they don't contain your very own mix of ingredients.

Equipment
Non-metallic bowl
Microwave (if melting the soap base using this method)
Microwave proof foil/wrap (if melting the soap base using this method)
Large saucepan (half filled with boiling water—only if using the double boiler method)
Heavy wooden or plastic spoon
Molds

Ingredients
Ready-made soap base
½ tsp (20 drops) essential oils of your choice (see pages 33–37)
Any dry ingredients you want (see pages 40–44)

Method

1. If you are melting your soap base in the microwave, place the mixture into the non-metallic bowl, cover with microwave-proof wrap, and heat on the highest setting for 30 seconds. Remove and stir using the wooden or plastic spoon, squashing any lumps to smooth the mixture. (If the soap base hasn't melted enough to allow you to stir, return the mixture to the microwave for a further 30 seconds.) Now heat the mixture on the lowest setting for about five minutes. The melting time will vary depending on the ingredients in the ready-made soap base so it is a good idea to

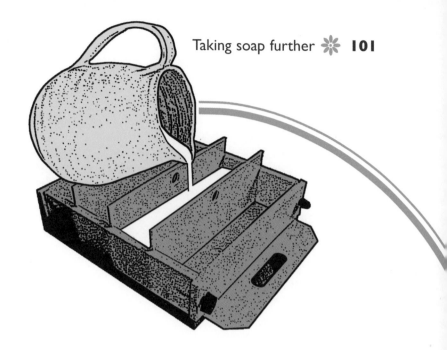

check the progress of the melting every so often by stirring the mixture. If you are using the double-boiler method, half fill the saucepan with boiling water, put your soap base into the non-metallic bowl, and place the bowl into the saucepan containing the boiling water. Cover with a tea towel and wait for the mixture to melt, stirring regularly to remove any lumps.

2. Once the mixture has thoroughly melted, you can add your choice of essential oils and dry ingredients.

3. Pour the soap into your mold and set the soap aside to cool for a few hours. Soaps made using this method do not need time to saponify or cure, nor do they need time to dry out, so once the soap has cooled it is ready to use.

Translucent soap

Translucent soap is generally not as kind to your skin as cold-processed soap so is best avoided if you have particularly sensitive skin. However, it can look great and makes a good hand soap.

Equipment
The same equipment is needed as for making cold-processed soap (see pages 45–47 for a list of general equipment), but you will also need the following additions:
Large glass or plastic jug
Large pan with a lid
Whisk
Electric hob
3 large glass or plastic jars
Heavy blanket
Heavy plastic sheeting
String or rope

Ingredients
1²/₃ cups sodium hydroxide crystals
3 cups distilled water
5 cups palm oil
2 cups coconut oil
3 cups castor oil
4¹/₂ cups ethanol
1 cup glycerin
Sugar solution (made from 1⁴/₅ cups distilled water and 3 cups sugar)
Ground spices for coloring (optional—see pages 40–44)
Few drops of essential oils of your choice (comprising no more than 3 percent of the total mixture—see pages 33–37)

SAFETY

Alcohol is highly flammable and for this reason it is not recommended that you use a gas stove. Be very careful when heating the alcohol and be sure to have a suitable fire extinguisher close by in case the mixture should ignite. Always wear gloves and goggles when working with alcohol.

A note on alcohol

This recipe contains ethanol which, at 190 percent proof, is a very strong grain alcohol. Ethanol can be bought from scientific or chemical suppliers and is usually denatured (so it can't be consumed). The type of denatured ethanol suitable for soap making is SDA 3A or SDA 3C. SDA stands for Specially Denatured Alcohol, and 3A is composed of 100 parts ethanol to 5 parts methyl alcohol while 3C is 100 parts ethanol to 5 parts isopropyl alcohol. If in any doubt, be sure to query this with your supplier as the wrong type of denatured ethanol can ruin your soap.

Method

1. Put on your goggles and gloves. Pour the sodium hydroxide crystals in your glass or plastic jug and place on a heat-proof surface in a well-ventilated area.

2. Add the measured water to the sodium hydroxide crystals while gently stirring all the time and taking care not to splash the solution. Keep your face well away from the jug at all times. Mix thoroughly to prevent the sodium hydroxide crystals from fusing into a white, solid mass which is hard to disperse.

3. Leave the solution to cool to 135–45°F, using a thermometer to check the temperature regularly. Meanwhile put the palm, coconut, and castor oils into the large pan and place over a gentle heat until their temperature also reaches 135–45°F.

4. When both mixtures are at the correct temperature, remove the pan from the heat and slowly pour the lye solution into the oil mixture, stirring all the time with a whisk. Be very careful not to splash the mixture as it is highly caustic.

5. Stir the soap vigorously with a wooden or plastic spoon, being careful not to allow too much air to get into the mix. Continue until the mixture reaches the trace stage (see page 59, step 8).

6. Place a lid over your pan and wrap the whole pan in the heavy blanket, securing it well. This allows saponification to take place at a high temperature, forming the transparent gel which becomes transparent soap. Leave to stand for one hour. Alternatively, you can speed the process up by placing the pan into a larger pan containing boiling water, shortening the saponification process to around 15 minutes. Put a couple of pieces of cutlery into the bottom of the larger pan with the boiling water to keep the pan containing the soap mixture as far away as possible from the direct heat.

7. Remove the blanket from the pan, if using, and the lid and check to see if the soap is translucent. If it is not, wrap it back in the blanket or return it to the pan of hot water until it becomes translucent. Stir the gelled soap for one minute with a whisk, making sure to scrape away the cooler soap from the sides and bottom of the pan. When it is thoroughly stirred, re-cover the soap and leave for one hour.

8. The soap should now have saponified and the temperature will have dropped as the chemical process ceases. Make sure your pan is on a flat surface and away from direct heat sources. Add the alcohol and the glycerin, taking note of the safety precautions given on page 103. The soap will still be warm and so will give off vapors when the ethanol is added—stand back and do not inhale this. Stir the mixture, scraping the hardening soap off the sides and bottom of the pan. Don't worry if it's lumpy as the lumps will dissolve later.

9. Cover the pan with the sheets of heavy plastic, securing with the string or rope. Secure tightly and gently pull the edges so that the plastic fits tightly, like the surface of a drum.

10. Place the covered pan into a larger pan half filled with boiling water to act as a double boiler (making sure the soap pan is not resting on the bottom of the larger pan, but has something under it, like some cutlery, to keep it away from the direct heat). Return the pan to the stove and heat gently until boiling point is reached. Boil the soap for about 30 minutes. The plastic will expand as air and steam are produced by the boiling soap mixture. If the plastic expands too much, remove the pan from the heat and pull the plastic tight again. Make sure the pan doesn't get so hot that it melts the plastic.

11. When the 30 minutes are nearly up, prepare your sugar solution. Bring the measured water to a boil and add the sugar. Stir until dissolved, then cover the pan, bring back to a boil, and simmer for two minutes.

12. Remove the soap pan from the heat and remove the plastic sheet. Add the sugar solution to the mixture. The sugar solution ensures a really clear soap, otherwise there is a tendency for the soap to become a bit cloudy.

13. Cover the pan and leave for around 20 minutes, until the temperature drops to 140°F. You can then add your ground spices and essential oils. The cooler the soap is when you add the essential oils, the stronger the scent will be.

14. Make sure your mold is well lined (see page 53) and that it is on a level surface where it can sit undisturbed for several hours. Pour the soap into your mold. If you have extra soap, pour it into small containers such as ice cube trays or margarine tubs for little quirky soap bars.

15. Once set, test that the soap is firm by pressing in the center of the soap and feeling for any give. You don't want to start taking it out of the mold only to find that the center is still runny!

16. Scrape off any residues and blemishes with your knife and then cut your soap into bars.

17. Place the bars on a shelf in a warm, well-ventilated room and cover with a light cloth. Leave for two weeks to cure. Your soap is now ready to enjoy!

Whipped soap

This soap is great fun to make and looks good too. The whipped texture is achieved by using a higher proportion of saturated fats than are included in a cold-processed soap.

Equipment
The same as for cold-processed soap (see pages 45–47) with the addition of a large mixing bowl and a whisk or an electric mixer with a whisk attachment.

Ingredients
⅔ cup cocoa butter
1 cup coconut oil
⁹⁄₁₀ cup palm oil
½ cup sodium hydroxide crystals
1 cup, 2 Tbsp distilled water
¾ cup olive oil
1–2 tsp (60-120 drops) of your chosen essential oils (see pages 33–37)

Method

1. Weigh the cocoa butter and coconut oil and place into the mixing bowl. Squash together with the back of a spoon as if you were creaming butter for a cake. If this is difficult you may want to soften the cocoa butter and coconut oil a little in the microwave before creaming.

2. Whisk the palm and olive oils together in a separate bowl until they resemble frothy egg white and form little peaks. (The more you mix, the frothier the oils will become, and the more "whipped" you soap will be.)

3. Slowly add the whisked oils to the cocoa butter and coconut oil mixture and whisk again to regain the fluffiness lost when the liquid oils were added.

4. Create your lye solution as for the cold-processed soap technique (see page 58, step 5) and allow it to cool at least to room temperature (the cooler the better so you might want to chill it). If the solution is too warm all of the bubbles you have whipped into your fats and oils will be lost.

5. Put on your gloves and goggles. Add the lye solution a few tablespoons at a time and continue whisking gently to avoid spills.

6. Continue whisking for a few more minutes. Add your essential oils and keep whisking until your mixture is the consistency of thick yogurt or whisked egg whites—you want a texture like meringue, where the sugar and egg whites form a heavy, creamy consistency.

7. Saponification will happen fairly slowly due to the mixture being at room temperature, allowing you more time to work with your soap. If you are using ground spices to color your soap, add them now and gently stir until well combined.

8. Pour your soap
into a lined mold (see page
53) or use a piping bag to pipe shapes
onto a tray lined with wax paper.

9. Lightly cover the mold or tray with a piece of cardboard and
place the soap in a warm room where there is good air circulation.

10. Leave the soap for 36 hours, allowing it time to harden (this is longer
than for cold-processed soap due to the lower temperatures used while
making the soap). Once the soap is hard, put your gloves on and remove
the soaps from the mold, if using, and place on a tray. If you wish to cut
your soaps, do this now.

11. Continue as for cold-processed soaps (see pages 60–61, steps 14, 15
and 16).

Liquid soaps

Liquid soaps are so convenient and sometimes just can't be replaced by their solid counterparts, so if you prefer these, and are able make them yourself, you will be even further along the road to self-sufficiency!

Equipment
Heat-proof jug
Sieve
Medium-sized, heavy-bottomed pan
Heat source
Heavy wooden or plastic mixing spoon
Large heat-proof bowl
Liquid soap dispenser
Stainless steel whisk

Ingredients for simple liquid soap
1 Tbsp potassium hydroxide in flake or pellet form (this is different from sodium hydroxide and is actually the kind of lye produced from wood ash and water)
⅗ cup distilled water
½ cup coconut oil
¾ tsp (40 drops) essential oils of your choice

Method for making simple liquid soap

1. Pour the potassium hydroxide into the heat-proof jug and add 4⅕ Tbsp of the distilled water. Set aside to cool to 80–100°F.

2. While the lye solution is cooling, heat the coconut oil and the remaining distilled water (4¾ Tbsp) in the pan over medium heat until the mixture reaches to 180°F. The oil and water will not completely mix until the next step.

3. Remove the pan from the heat and pour the lye solution slowly into the oil mixture, stirring gently.

4. Put the pan back on the heat and bring the mixture back up to 180°F. Stir continuously and do not allow the mixture to get any hotter than this temperature.

5. After 15 minutes the mixture should be a gel-like liquid. Before it starts to gel any further, pour it into the heat-proof bowl. Cover and leave for 24 hours to cool and solidify. If you wish, the soap can be stored at this stage for up for 12 weeks.

6. Put the soap in a pan and add one cup water. Heat the soap and water over low heat without stirring, gently pressing the soap into the water using a heavy wooden or plastic spoon (stirring creates lather that you don't want). Add your chosen essential oils at this point.

7. Once the soap and water have blended to a uniform consistency, carefully strain the mixture into a jug using the sieve and then pour your mixture into the liquid soap dispenser. The soap is now ready for use!

Ingredients for pearlescent liquid soap

1¼ Tbsp sugar
½ cup distilled water
¼ cup potassium hydroxide (in flake or pellet form)
½ cup coconut oil
1½ Tbsp castor oil
1 Tbsp vegetable glycerin
½ tsp (20 drops) essential oils of your choice

Method for making pearlescent liquid soap

1. Bring 6 Tbsp of the distilled water to a boil and dissolve the sugar in it. Set the sugar solution aside.

2. Put on your gloves and goggles. Dissolve the potassium hydroxide in the remaining 2 Tbsp of distilled water. Set the lye solution aside.

3. Heat the coconut oil over low heat. Once melted, add the castor oil and set the pan aside to cool. Slowly add the lye solution to the oils, gently whisking all the time until the soap reaches trace stage (see page 59, step 8).

4. Return the pan to the heat and bring up to 120°F. Add the glycerin while stirring continuously.

5.   Reheat the sugar solution to somewhere between 140 and 150°F.

6.   Add the sugar solution to the soap, mixing gently all the time, and heat the mixture to 160°F.

7.   Allow the soap to sit for ten minutes.

8.   Whisk the mixture thoroughly—as it will have separated—then put the bowl in the fridge and whisk every 5 or 10 minutes until the soap is cool and well blended.

9.   Pour the soap into a suitable container, cover, and leave it to sit for 24 hours.

10.   Return the soap mixture to a heavy pan and heat gently, adding enough water to create the desired consistency (add the water little-by-little so that you don't add too much).

11.   Add your essential oils and pour the mixture into a liquid soap dispenser. Your soap is now ready to enjoy.

Fun ideas for creative soap

There are lots of entertaining things you can do with soap, from recycling scraps to creating fun shapes for kids. Get creative and make bath time a real treat. Anything goes, from just plain frivolous to ultra-practical.

Tingly, re-milled mint soap

Make a bar of re-milled soap (see pages 98–99), adding a small handful of spirulina and a few drops each of peppermint and eucalyptus essential oils. As the soap does not need to saponify, the essential oils retain their scent and give you a really zingy soap that is very popular with the boys—they seem to like a good, hearty soap that smells strong! The spirulina also stays even greener when it doesn't go through the saponification process, so you get a minty-green food bar for your skin.

Fun kids soap

You can sculpt cold-processed soap at the stage you would pour it into a mold, or you can use re-milled soap (pages 98–99). Wearing gloves (especially if you are using soap you have just made, rather than re-milled, as it is still a little caustic), take a palm-full of soap and sculpt it into round balls, larger rocks, animals, shapes, or anything else you like. Unscented, re-milled soap is great for making fun shapes for kids. Once the soap is melted, separate it into three bowls and add orange essential oil to one along with a few drops of natural red and yellow food coloring (not too much or it will turn your kids orange when they wash with it!); add lime essential oil to the second, along with a few drops of natural green food coloring; and add lemon essential oil to the third along with a few drops of natural yellow food coloring.

Then, wearing gloves to stop the color from dying your hands, create little (or large) fruit shapes from the three colors to really add fun to bath times!

Toy surprise

While your soap is still soft, press a small toy into the center of each bar and press the soap around it again to cover it. This will give the kids a lovely surprise and encourage them to use the soap to reach the toy. Make sure you don't use anything with sharp edges that will scratch delicate skin—you want to encourage them to wash, not put them off!

Exfoliating bath rocks

Using re-milled soap, add lots of ground pumice to some of your mixture as it is starting to set and mold it into a rock shape. Try and press the soap together as it cools and dries so you get a nice, tightly-packed soap. You can then use this soap in the same way you would use a pumice stone, as it will be really gritty and exfoliating.

Loofah slice soap

Take a long loofah with a hollow center and slice it into pieces (as if slicing a baguette). Use these slices as little molds and fill each slice with the soap of your choice (you will need to cover one end of each slice with plastic-wrap pulled tight around the outside and taped securely, otherwise the soap will pour out the bottom when you fill it). This is a great way to use up leftovers from a soap batch if you have made too much for your usual molds, or for re-milled scraps.

Soap on a rope

Dangle a rope, as heavy or thin as you like, in your chosen soap mold. Try and get the rope to hang in the middle of the container and fasten it to a pencil or spoon at the other end so it stays put, then pour in your soap. A great mix of essential oils for re-milled soap is eucalyptus and mint. As the soap is already saponified, when you add essential oils the scent stays a lot stronger so you end up with a more strongly-scented soap.

Chunky translucent soap

Gather together some soap odds and ends, or slice and grate a new bar of nice, brightly-colored soap. Sprinkle the pieces of soap around your soap mold. Make a batch of translucent soap (see pages 102–103) and pour this into the molds with the pieces of ready-made soap. This will create pretty, patterned soaps with a kind of stained-glass effect. You can also make this soap with cold-processed soap—your colored scraps will show through a little less but will become more visible as you use the soap. Or you can get a translucent melt-and-pour base and use this if you don't want to make your own translucent soap. The possibilities are almost endless!

Loofah scrub

Chop some loofah into little pieces and add it to your soap at the trace stage, along with your essential oils and other dry ingredients. This creates an exfoliating soap—how scrubby it is depends on how big you make the loofah pieces.

Bits and pieces

Why not add fresh
mint to your
mint soap,
finely grated
orange rind to
your orange soap,
flecks of lemon rind
to your lemon soap,
and so on? This is a great way
of using up fresh ingredients
lurking in your fridge or fruit bowl.

If you have some milk that needs using up but don't have the time to make a milk soap, try making some re-milled soap and replacing a portion of the water in the recipe with milk. Or make a milk and honey soap by making a paste from one tablespoon milk and one tablespoon honey. Mix them together before adding to the soap mix along with your essential oils. (Don't try adding powdered milk at the same time as your essential oils—the saponification process can do strange things to powdered milk!)

Rather than throwing flowers away once they are past their best, why not dry the petals or buds and press them into your soap once it begins to harden to add a decorative, floral touch? This works best in re-milled soap as saponification does tend to turn things brown. I have had lovely, pink rose buds turn a rusty shade of brown in some soaps—not so pretty after all!

Painting

You can buy natural pigment paints to use on your soaps which are kind to your skin and are safe for any children. Get creative and paint whatever you like. This is a great way to personalize soaps to be given as gifts.

Homemade skin care

Now that you have so many great ingredients at your fingertips you have the raw materials to make lots of simple, natural skin-care products. Here are just a few ideas to get you started. You'll be amazed what you can whip up in a few minutes!

Soap scrap squid

Grate your old soap scraps and mix them with some fresh or dried lavender, rosemary, mint, thyme, or whatever herbs you like, chopping the herbs up first so they don't poke anyone through the flannel! Then get a brightly-colored flannel and stitch some eyes onto it with embroidery thread, cotton thread, or wool, or use small buttons (not for small children though). Fill the flannel about half-full with your soap and herb mix and secure with a piece of embroidery thread, wool, or ribbon so that the mixture is bunched up at the top and the rest of the flannel hangs down like tentacles. Enjoy bathtime with your very own sea squid!

Cleopatra's bath salts

A delicious, rejuvenating, and moisturizing bath salt mix can be made using ingredients you probably have in your kitchen cupboard. Combine two tablespoons of table salt with a tablespoon of powdered milk, a capful of vanilla essence, and four drops of neroli essential oil to create a luxurious, indulgent bath. The salt will encourage circulation in the skin and draw toxins from the body, while the milk works to nourish and replenish, making sure you don't come out looking like a prune!

If you would like to create a more adventurous bath salt mix, try to get your hands on some Dead Sea salt (available from good pharmacies), which is universally renowned for its beneficial qualities. The therapeutic effects of bathing in the Dead Sea were known centuries ago, and Cleopatra would even request salt from the Dead Sea for her baths. Today, modern science has found truth in the claims of Dead Sea salt's healing qualities, showing that the minerals and vitamins contained in the salt can have a wonderful effect on numerous skin conditions as well as rheumatism.

It is reputed that to bathe in epsom salts relieves pain, and in the past epsom salts were thought to have magical healing properties. This salt is made up primarily of magnesium sulphate. Magnesium is one of the most important minerals in the body. In a bath containing epsom salts, magnesium is absorbed through the skin, and this can help to increase circulation and ease aches and pains. Magnesium has both anti-inflammatory and antiarthritic properties.

To get the best out of an epsom or Dead Sea salts bath, add a cup of each to a hot bath and have a long, relaxing soak. You might want to add a couple drops of clary sage, lavender, or thyme essential oils if you have aching muscles.

Emollient face scrub

To make a quick and easy face scrub, finely grate some soap, mix with whichever herbs you like, and add some oats or oatmeal. Apply to the skin and rub! This is a rather messy face scrub so make sure you put the plug in the sink before you start using it or you might block up the plumbing. You could put the mixture inside a folded flannel and use this as a scrubbing pad, releasing the qualities of the soap, herbs, and oats onto your skin without making too much mess.

Solid moisturizing bar

Did you know...

...that you can keep your Solid Moisturizing Bar in the fridge or freezer and slice bits off when you want to use them? This can feel lovely for a massage on a hot day, or to soothe sun burned skin.

You can make a quick moisturizing bar by combining cocoa butter with coconut oil. You could also add shea butter or mango butter for added nourishing qualities, replacing a portion of the coconut oil with these. I have found that this works best if the mixture is made up of 20 percent soft butters and coconut oil and 80 percent cocoa butter, but do play around to see what consistency you like best. Gently melt the cocoa butter in a pan, making sure to keep the temperature as low as possible. When it is nearly melted, remove the pan from the heat and add the other butters—they will melt in the warm pan. Pour the mixture into a bowl and stir until cool. Add your essential oils and remember to add some grapefruit seed extract as a preservative. Keep stirring until the mixture starts to thicken and then pour in your molds. You may want to speed up the thickening by sitting your bowl in a larger bowl of cold water. Be sure to stir continuously though or it will harden around the edges of the bowl. Individual molds work best, as this mixture is difficult to cut once it hardens and tends to shatter. The plastic trays you get cookies in are good molds, as are ice-cube trays for smaller bars.

Bath melts

These wonderfully indulgent melts can be made with pure shea
butter. The key is to make them small—about the size of a boiled candy.
A flexible ice-cube tray is a great mold for these and you get some fun
shapes too. Melt some shea butter gently over low heat. Add a few drops
of your chosen essential oil—neroli and ylang ylang are really heady and
luxurious scents—and a few drops of grapefruit seed extract or another
natural preservative (Vitamin E oil or rosemary extract). Pour your
mixture into a bowl and keep stirring until it starts to thicken and set (you
can place your bowl in a sink of cold water to quicken this process if you
like). Watch for the mixture starting to solidify on the edges of the bowl
and pour into molds when it does. Leave to set overnight. You can press
dried flower petals into the outside of your melts if you like, or when they
are set carefully, mold them into balls (they are quite soft) and then roll
them in petals—both look really pretty.

Bath tea bags

Create a little muslin bag, like a tea-bag made of material, and fill your bag
with dried or fresh herbs and oats. Tie the bag shut and hang it over the
hot-tap while your bath is running. The hot water will draw out the
properties of the herbs and the emollient qualities of the oats, creating an
indulgent and skin-caring bath. You can leave the bag hanging in your bath
while you bathe, if you like, for a more intense effect.

Almond face-and-body scrub

Ground almonds are rich in protein, zinc, potassium, iron, B vitamins, and
magnesium, as well as almond oil. Gently massaging this nutritious nut on
your skin allows the epidermis to absorb some of the many nutrients and
be conditioned by the oil. The paste also softens and exfoliates dead skin
cells, resulting in a cleaner, clearer complexion. This is great for spotty
teenage skin as it is gentle and doesn't strip the skin of its natural oils like

so many acne-controlling products on the market. Use ground almonds on damp skin as a rich and gentle face-and-body scrub or add a drop or two of peppermint essential oil for a foot scrub to revive hot and tired feet.

Rosemary rinse for glossy locks

Rosemary is traditionally associated with hair. It has been said that it strengthens the hair and stimulates the scalp, and rosemary essential oil is thought to stimulate the mind and alieve fatigue. Rosemary also helps to discourage dandruff and it makes your hair smell good too! Put a few sprigs of fresh rosemary in a heat-proof bowl and pour boiling water over to cover. Allow the herb to infuse the water and, when cool, strain to remove the rosemary. Use the rosemary water as a final rinse to keep hair glossy and sleek. You can put the rest of the infusion into a pretty glass bottle and keep in the fridge, or somewhere out of direct light, for later use.

Nettle-vinegar rinse for dandruff

Wearing gloves to avoid sticks, pick a handful of nettles and place in a heat-proof bowl. Pour in two cups of boiling water and leave overnight. Strain to remove the nettles and add a cup of cider vinegar to the nettle infusion. Use your nettle and vinegar solution as a final rinse for your hair, making sure you pour it over the scalp well. This is a great hair tonic, giving you lovely, glossy locks as well as keeping dandruff at bay. Vinegar helps to cleanse the hair, removing any residue and build-up from shampoo and minerals contained in tap water. Removing these residues allows the hair's cuticles to sit smoothly, creating light-reflective, gorgeous hair. You can either use your rinse right away or pour into dark glass or plastic bottles

Did you know...
...that using vinegar combined with plant extracts or essential oils for cosmetic purposes dates back to the Romans, and was also fashionable during the 1800s as "vinaigre de toilette."

and store in the fridge or out of direct sunlight. It will last longer in the fridge, but remember natural creations like this have no artificial preservatives, so it is probably best to use them within a week or so.

Flower petal tea

This one's not for your skin but is nice, natural, and simple and great for drinking while you relax in the bath with one of your luxurious, homemade soaps. Add fresh or dried rose or jasmine petals to a pot of good-quality green or black leaf tea. Get into your bath, lay back, and enjoy. You can also use mint, or any other herb or flower you know to be edible and beneficial for your health—but it is better if it tastes good or you probably won't drink it!

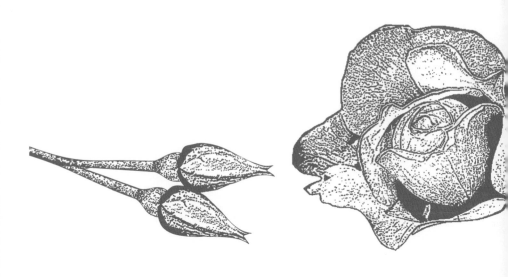

SAPONIFICATION CHART

Multiply the amount of oil you are using in ounces by the value for that oil from the chart. This gives the amount of sodium hydroxide needed to make soap with that oil. (This chart does not work for potassium hydroxide—you will need to find the saponification values for that as they are different to those for sodium hydroxide.)

To work out how much water you will need for your soap recipe, it is easiest to work from the recipes listed in this book—work out the caustic soda-to-water ratio used and then transfer that to your new recipe. In most soap making, it is generally around ⅓ sodium hydroxide to water ratio. As you will see from our recipes, this is not exactly the proportion we use, but we have found the amount of water which works best for our soaps. Water does not actually take part in the saponification process—it just acts as a solvent and allows the thorough dispersal of sodium hydroxide throughout the soap mixture. Although water is not an active ingredient—so you don't have to be quite as precise with its proportions as you do with the caustic soda and oil measurements—too much water can mean your soap will turn out soft and too little water can create a dry, caustic soap.

almond oil	0.136	borage oil	0.136
apricot seed oil	0.135	Brazil nut oil	0.175
avocado oil	0.133	butterfat (cow)	0.162
bayberry or myrtle oil	0.069	butterfat (goat)	0.167
bear fat, bear tallow	0.139	camelia oil	0.136
beef hoof oil, neat's foot oil	0.141	carnauba wax	0.069
beef tallow	0.140	castor oil	0.128
beeswax	0.069	chicken fat	0.138

cocoa butter	0.137	niger-seed oil	0.135
coconut oil	0.190	olive oil	0.134
cod liver oil	0.132	palm oil	0.141
coffee-seed oil	0.130	palm-seed oil, palm butter	0.156
corn oil, maize oil	0.136
cottonseed oil	0.138	peanut oil, groundnut oil	0.136
Chinese vegetable tallow	0.135	pistachio oil	0.135
deer tallow, vension fat	0.139	poppy seed oil	0.138
emu oil/fat, ostrich oil/fat	0.135	pumpkin seed oil	0.135
evening primrose oil	0.136	rapeseed oil	0.124
flax seed oil, linseed oil	0.135	rice bran oil	0.128
goat tallow, goat fat	0.139	castor oil	0.128
goose fat	0.136	safflower oil	0.136
grapefruit seed oil	0.123 to 0.135	sardine oil	0.135
		sesame seed oil	0.133
hazelnut oil	0.136	shea butter, African karite butter	0.128
hemp seed oil	0.1375
herring oil	0.136	sheep tallow	0.138
jojoba oil	0.069	soybean oil	0.135
kukui oil, candle nut oil	0.135	sunflower seed oil	0.134
lanolin, sheep wool fat	0.074	vegetable oil shortening, hydrogenated vegetable oil	0.136
pork tallow/fat	0.138
linseed oil, flax seed oil	0.136	walnut oil	0.136
macademia nut oil	0.139	whale: sperm whale, body, blubber oil, short oil	0.092
margarine	0.136
mink oil	0.140	whale: sperm whale, head	0.102
mustard seed oil	0.123	whale: baleen whale	0.138
neem oil	0.138	wheat germ oil	0.132

For a list of U.S. retailers catering to all your soap making needs, please check out these websites:

www.tanela.com/cat/supplies/retail/soapmaking.html

www.wholesaleworld.us/wholesale_soap_and_candle_making_supplies.php